Chinese art and identity

A BRUSH WITH POWER

HONG KONG

What a medieval work of calligraphy tells you about contemporary China

SOME TIME in the fourth century, a politician called Wang Xizhi gathered 42 friends at the beautiful Orchid Pavilion on Mount Kuaiji in what is now eastern Zhejiang province in China. The men floated lotus-leaf cups filled with rice wine down a stream. When a goblet stopped, the nearest guest had to drink and write a poem. The drunken Wang was delighted at the ensuing literary outpouring. So he wrote a preface to the collection. In 324 characters Wang, who was acclaimed for his skill in calligraphy, expressed joy at the ensemble and melancholy at such fleeting happiness.

Calligraphy has for two millennia been considered the highest form of art in China. Wang's screed is one of the finest and most famous examples. The original, completed in 353AD, is long vanished. But Wang inspired others, as he was inspired. Many duplicated his preface, imitating his brushstrokes precisely. One came up at an auction at Sotheby's in Hong Kong in October, consisting of copies by Emperors Renzong and Gaozong, Song dynasty rulers from the 11th and 12th centuries. The endless iterations of the Orchid Pavilion preface are both an emblem of Chinese culture, and a lens through which China views its past.

In imperial China, prowess with a brush was a mark of refinement, like piano-playing in Victorian Britain. But it was also a sign of moral strength. "Beware a man whose writing sways like a reed in the wind," Confucius, China's most famous philosopher, cautioned in 500BC. But the test was not just of one's handling of a brush, but of imitating the master. In this, as Robert Harrist junior of Columbia University puts it, Chinese calligraphy is "copies, all the way down".

Replicating classic works showed your allegiance to Confucian values, key among them accordance with hierarchy, at the top of which sat the emperor. Brush work was part of the imperial exams for prospective government officials. The Orchid Pavilion preface was often the subject. Its use as a symbol of loyalty extended to the highest office. In the scroll being auctioned, Gaozong's work was a gift to a senior minister, to show that, even as the Song dynasty crumbled and his territory shrank, he was the legitimate heir to its history.

Each successive owner of the scroll stamped their possession on the front of the artwork with a crimson ▸▸

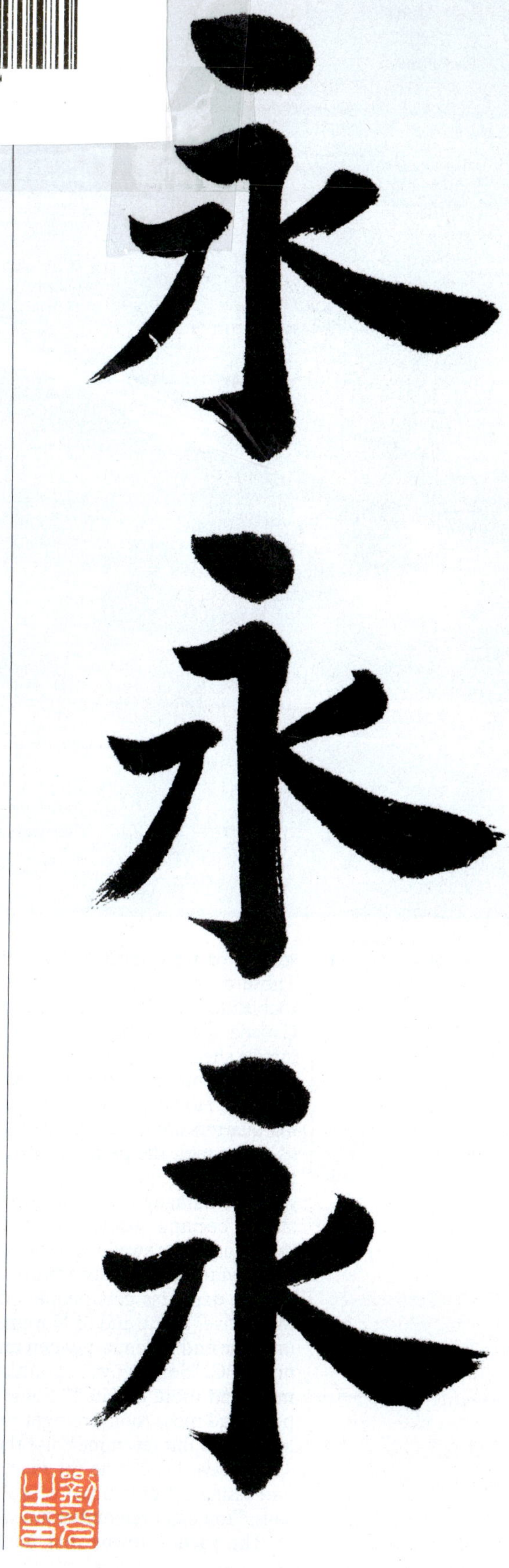

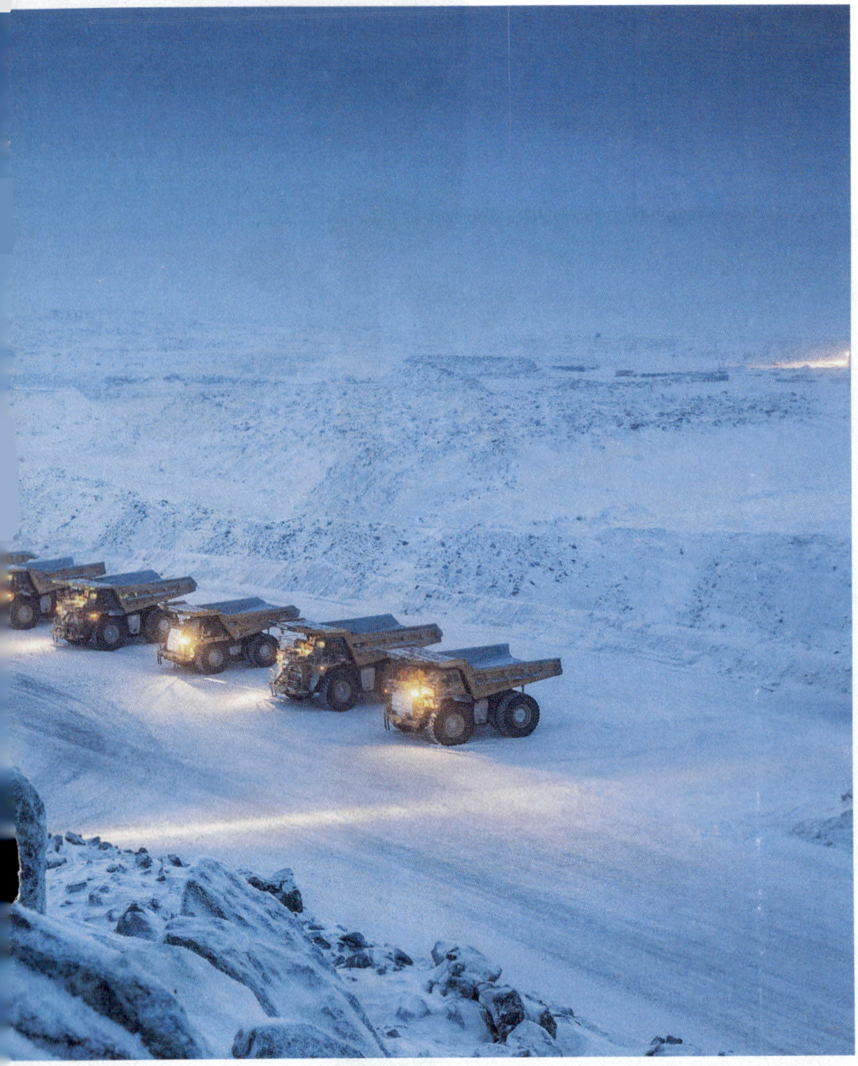

scurvy, or were reduced to eating their own boots. Those days have passed, but in 2024 miners died in rock slides and floods in Russia and a plane crash in Canada. The number of people falling through melting ice sheets has also risen.

Good employers strain to keep workers safe, which is costly. Housing must often be designed so that living quarters are warm but the foundations are cool, so as not to melt the permafrost (frozen tundra). Softening it can trigger slumps (a kind of landslide). In August the Batagay Crater in Russia, the world's largest slump, became visible from space. Since opening in the 1960s, it has swallowed surface land the width of 14 Giza pyramids (roughly 3.2km).

The darkness gets people down. The sun sets on Mary River at the end of November, and does not rise until the end of January, when temperatures fall to minus 60°C. "Some guys", says Alan, a worker, "just get more and more deflated." Some mines have installed pools and mess rooms to fight the claustrophobia and loneliness. But few miners use them, says Alan, as long shifts leave little time for much other than sleeping and eating. After 12 hours of isolation, another worker says, "You can't remember how to talk to people."

No light, no warmth, no women. Good wages, though

The pseudo-towns that house miners across the Arctic have a strict no-alcohol policy to avoid accidents. Staff are searched for contraband at the airfield. But "a little bootlegging" happens anyway, Alan says.

Arctic employers would love to attract more female staff, but few want to work in a frozen wasteland. Agnico Eagle, Canada's biggest mining company, reckons only 15% of its workforce are women. This normal for the industry—the atmosphere in Arctic camps is rather macho. Kathy Lane, a woman who used to work at Deadhorse, an oil complex in Alaska, is reluctant to get into specifics. "Let's just say everyone knew who you were, but the men got to stay anonymous."

Commercial mine workers are flown in and out every fortnight. (Alan spends his time off in Florida, gorging on sunshine.) The productivity of fly-in, fly-out workers is low, however. Canadian Arctic construction workers are a third less effective than their counterparts down south, found a study in 2023 from the University of Western Australia. This may be because the lifestyle makes them glum. And perhaps also because they are under-managed. Since it is impossible to bring families to the camp, almost no one's boss lives on site, so easy fixes often go unnoticed.

The men in exploration camps, who take samples before commercial mining begins, are the most isolated of all. Nathan, Connor and Eg, the three geologists with the coyote problem, were dropped with three helicopter-loads of kit at a camp in Canada's Northwest Territories in March. They have barely left since.

Between the coyote, the storms and the summer wildfires, there have been plenty of bad days, costing their employer a bundle of cash. But on a good day, the wilderness is glorious and the mood is lively. The men control their own timetable, unlike at a tightly scheduled mine, and booze is allowed. Working here is a little more dangerous, and a little more fun.

Many of these men (and every explorer *The Economist* met was male) have been bouncing around remote spots for a long time. "Greenland, Australia, Zambia, Congo," says Connor, "and now here." They bring their own kit, and can make $300,000 for a long season. Unlike mine workers, few have families.

All eight Arctic governments prop up polar business. The state is the biggest employer in Canada's three northern provinces, and public subsidies outstrip mining revenues. Greenland gets two-thirds of its income from the Danish state. Russia subsidises a coal mine to buttress its spurious claim to parts of Svalbard, a Norwegian archipelago.

The Arctic resource rush has, unsurprisingly, affected the nearest towns. In Whitehorse, the capital of Canada's Yukon province, property prices have soared as outsiders pour in. Mining firms, eager to soothe the local First Nation (indigenous) population, offer lots of jobs but find few takers. At a job fair run by Kwanlin Dun, a First Nation group, only 20 jobseekers turned up to meet 200 would-be employers. Most young locals already have jobs, says Adrienne Hill, a First Nation spokesperson, and few think the trade-off of more money for grim working conditions is worth it.

Besides, as in previous gold rushes all over the world, there is money to be made providing services for miners, from selling shovels and steaks to leasing helicopters and tow trucks. There is an old Greenlandic saying: "We do not care if they find anything, as long as they keep looking." They surely will. ●

seal. What might be considered vandalism on a Western painting merely adds to the price of this one. The value ascribed to having a visible chain of owners is a further indication that, when it comes to calligraphy, continuity and conformity are prized over originality.

Many artefacts and practices of imperial rule were destroyed after the communists came to power in 1949, but calligraphy endured. Mao Zedong was proud of his own hand. His four-character calligraphy still stands at the masthead for *People's Daily*, the flagship party mouthpiece. He weighed in on academic debates about Wang's Orchid Pavilion preface. In fact, the Cultural Revolution was arguably the heyday of popular calligraphy. Red guards plastered city streets with posters daubed with characters denouncing fellow citizens, and brush shops thrived.

STROKES OF FORTUNE

The importance of calligraphy has only grown, even beyond the mainland, where China is eager to enhance its soft power. When Erin Chan was growing up in Hong Kong, in the 1980s, learning English was the passport to success. Ms Chan says she "did not dare" to tell her friends that she loved drawing characters. These days her passion stands her in good stead. She runs classes for students of all ages at the Pinzi Calligraphy Studio, and teaches in schools. Why is the craft in fashion now? Parents are "very realistic", she says.

The revival or invention of traditions often reveals much about the anxieties of the present. As China's leader since 2012, Xi Jinping has transformed calligraphy from an art form to a cultural practice that conforms to and boosts the version of the country's history promoted by the Chinese Communist Party (CCP).

Today children in Chinese schools must study calligraphy from age six to fifteen. Lessons are called art classes, but self-expression and creativity are discouraged. In 2018 students taking the *gaokao*, China's competitive university-entrance exam, stopped getting bonus points for maths, sports and science. They get extra credit only for art, which includes calligraphy.

The elevation of calligraphy is part of a wider government-backed drive to build what Mr Xi labels "cultural confidence": a pride in being Chinese that unites people and presents the CCP as the ultimate defender of China's unique qualities. The state broadcaster launched a popular national programme, "Chinese Spelling Hero", in which children paint complex characters. An adult version also aired. Government-sponsored "art" competitions offer cash prizes.

Calligraphy is used to promote unity outside mainland China, too. In September the CCP staged a mass calligraphy event in Hong Kong for people to express their "heartfelt blessings...for the great motherland". In a brazen denial of the CCP's destructive history, Mr Xi is reigniting Chinese traditions to secure the party's role as "faithful heir" to China's glorious past and as a protector of its uniqueness against "foreign forces".

The CCP presents calligraphy as an enduring sign of nationhood. After the fall of the Qing, China's final dynasty, in the early 20th century, some intellectuals proposed abandoning pictographic writing, saying that it held the new nation back from advancing in science and logic. They failed. The 8,000 characters used in mainland China have been simplified since 1949,

Replicating classic works showed your allegiance to Confucian values

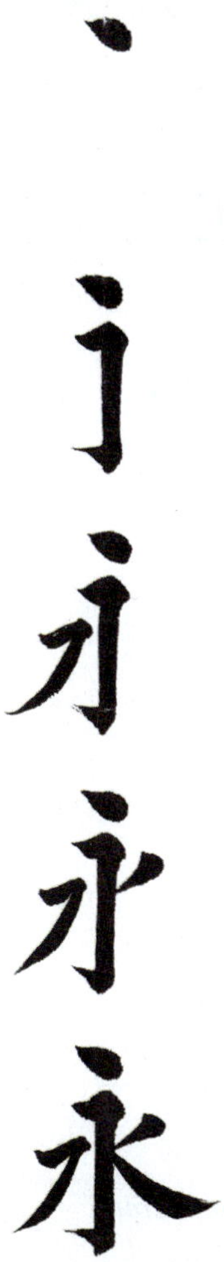

but have stuck. Students still practise the first character of Wang's preface, *yong*, "forever" (pictured).

And at the Man Luen Choon art-supply shop in Hong Kong, many items would be familiar to Wang. They include the "four treasures" of Chinese calligraphy: brush, paper, inkstone and ink. Most of the ink on sale is still black, as in the fourth century. Beside brushes made from goat-beard, rabbit hair and "auspicious dragon wolf" sit hard, weasel-hair wands like the one Renzong would have used a thousand years ago.

But the CCP's insistence that calligraphy reflects Chinese unity is a revision of the past. For most of their history, those who live in today's China spoke hundreds of mutually incomprehensible dialects and languages. Steven Zuo, an expert on Chinese paintings at Sotheby's, notes that Wang's preface, if recited by someone in Song territory, would have been unintelligible to someone from elsewhere in the empire.

Chinese script was used by scholars to communicate because they would otherwise have been unable to understand each other. Until the mid-20th century, the written language, including all forms of calligraphy, replaced a shared spoken tongue, as Latin did in medieval Europe. And like Latin, calligraphy was inaccessible to most. When Mao proclaimed the People's Republic, only 20% of people in the country were literate, maybe less, at a time when 97% of Americans and Britons, were and 49% of Brazilians.

The presentation of writing as culture in China has led to an unusual emphasis on its importance to claims about national heritage. Mr Xi boasts of "5,000 years of unbroken Chinese civilisation". Yet the earliest inscriptions date from the Shang dynasty, around 1600BC. Trying to find the oldest records, the state has ploughed money into archaeology, particularly in the past decade. No such traces have been uncovered.

That has left the CCP with two problems. First, the accolade for the oldest writing goes to the Sumerians of ancient Mesopotamia (now Iraq), where cuneiform script was used in around 3,200BC. The second, deeper problem, is that writing is considered a fundamental part of what denotes a civilisation: without earlier records, the party's claim of 5,000 years looks wobbly.

The answer has been to change the definition of civilisation. The CCP has done this before. "Democracy" means the party, which perfectly represents the people. "Human rights" means economic development, not freedom. "Civilisation" has been given the same treatment. In September a CCP-sponsored exhibition entitled "The Origins of Chinese Civilisation" opened in Hong Kong. "What is civilisation?" asks the opening text. Its answer rejects the "international academic criteria" based on "writing, metallurgy and cities". Instead it offers "the Chinese criteria for defining civilisation", which includes population, social stratification and the emergence of class. Chinese academics have made similar arguments.

In Hong Kong bids for the Song-dynasty scroll reached HK$95m but it did not make its reserve price. A private buyer may nab it. Across the city the M+ gallery is showing the work of Qiu Zhijie, an artist from Fujian, replicating the Orchid Pavilion preface in a video installation. He copies it a thousand times on a single sheet of rice paper. As Mr Qiu's brush progresses, the text becomes illegible, "losing meaning and historical significance": a true character statement. ●

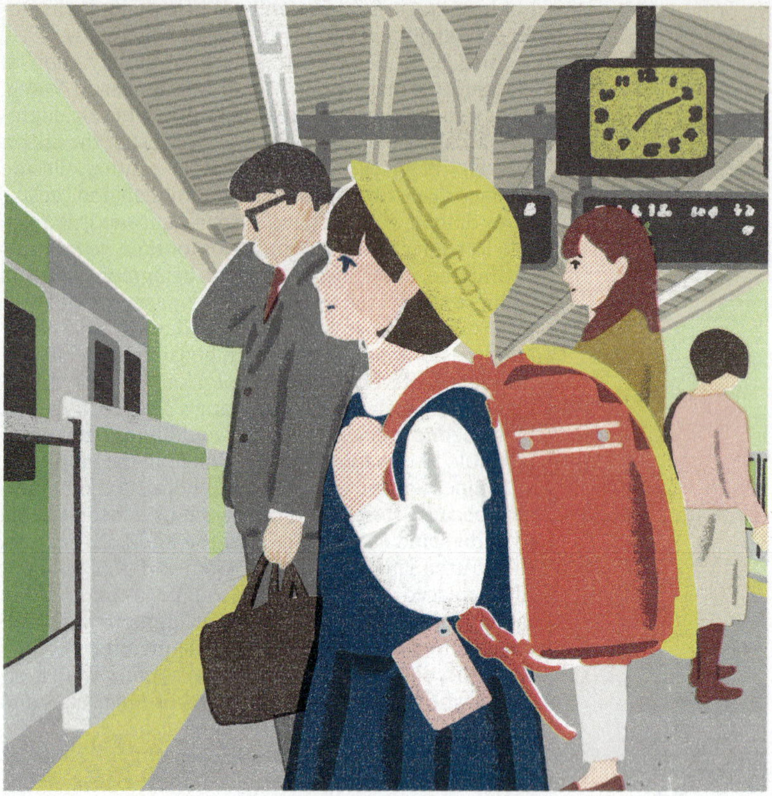

Inside the world's most disciplined primary schools

THE JAPANESE ART OF CHILD-REARING

TOKYO AND MEXICO CITY

Why are small kids in Japan so capable and considerate? And what is the downside?

WHY DOES Ohtani Shohei, a Japanese baseball star, pick up litter after games? Why do Japanese people queue so politely, and wait for green lights before crossing the road? Why, in short, is Japan so orderly? Some say the answer lies in its primary schools.

As the final bell rings, a flurry of six- and seven-year-olds dash out of class at Minami Ikebukuro Primary School in Tokyo: hats on, water bottles flying. Four girls are left behind; it's their turn to clean up. They pull child-sized brooms from a cupboard and get to work. Four brushes knock together as they gather paper shreds and dirt. "It always gets dusty here," says Mariya, pointing to grooves in the floor. The others rush over to help. By cleaning, children learn not to make a mess in the first place, says Kohashiguchi Megumi, the teacher. They also learn to be egalitarian: no, "Oh the caretaker will clean it up later."

At first, small children "act wild, like monsters!" says Satou Hiroshi, the genial head teacher. "Our job is to prepare them to enter society" by teaching them to collaborate, take initiative and treat everyone equally. He calls it *hito-zukuri*, the art of making people.

The results are impressive. Not only do Japanese children do well academically; they also show remarkable independence at a young age. Six-year-olds walk or ride the metro unaccompanied to school. (It helps that the country is unusually safe.) Sugiura Kouma, seven, walks the ten-minute route daily. "I get nervous because he has to cross a main road, but people help him," says Hiroki, his father. A Japanese reality show features toddlers going to the shops on their own to buy fishcakes. Contrast this with the hysterical safety-ism sometimes seen in the West, where many parents are convinced something terrible will happen if they stop hovering over their children for an instant, and where governments sometimes act as if this were true. In October Brittany Patterson, a mother in the American state of Georgia, was handcuffed and arrested because her 10-year-old was seen walking calmly to the town less than a mile from his home.

Your correspondent takes a particular interest in Japanese education: her children attended pre-school in Tokyo, when she was *The Economist*'s bureau chief there, and are now at a Japanese school in Mexico. Over the years, she has seen both the strengths of the system, such as imbuing children with self-discipline and consideration for others, and its flaws, such as excessive conformity. This article stems, in part, from the debate within her family about how long to stick with Japanese-style schooling. To assess the system fairly, she went back to Japan to investigate.

Japan's approach dates back centuries. During the feudal Edo period (1603-1868), the samurai class set up schools to train literate, ethical warriors. Schools in temples trained the peasants; this may be where the practice of kids cleaning classrooms began. In the 19th century, after the shock of contact with the industrialised West, education was centralised and geared to modernisation. As Japan turned to militarism in the 20th century, schools promoted imperial fervour. After defeat in the second world war and American occupation, the curriculum became more democratic.

Schools in Japan today still strive to build character. They stress discipline and responsibility to others, says Nakano Koichi, a political scientist. Group harmony trumps individualism. Authority is important. ▸▸

Chinese Calligraphy

Standard script for beginners

中國書法

楷書初步

Introduction
Jane Portal

Text and calligraphy
Qu Lei Lei

ARTMEDIA RESOURCES

Published in association with The British Museum Press
by Art Media Resources Inc
1507 South Michigan Avenue Chicago IL 60605
www.artmediaresources.com

ISBN 1–58886–071–X

Designed by Mustafa Ja'far
Cover calligraphy by Qu Lei Lei
Front cover: 'The way' (*dao*)
Back cover: 'If you want to see further, climb up higher'
Typeset in Humanist
Printed in Great Britain by Goodman Baylis Ltd

Introduction

Although Chinese is spoken by more people in the world than any other language, there are many different regional dialects which are incomprehensible to people living outside the particular region. However, the Chinese script is the same regardless of the dialect, and this unites the Chinese-speaking world. In fact, it also embraces neighbouring countries such as Japan, Korea and Vietnam, all of which originally used Chinese script but which have now developed writing systems of their own, sometimes mixed with Chinese characters.

The earliest Chinese script was written on animal bones and tortoise shells from around the thirteenth to the eleventh century BC and recorded questions asked of the gods on behalf of the ruler. The bones were then heated and the resulting cracks interpreted to provide the answers to the questions. These characters incorporate pictograms and are irregular and quite unlike modern Chinese script. The next type of script was that inscribed on bronze ritual vessels from about the eleventh to the eighth century BC. First incised in clay moulds before the bronze was cast, texts in this script often record the reasons for the donation of the bronze to the owner.

When the first emperor of China, Qin Shihuangdi, unified China in 221 BC, he standardized the different forms of writing to create a regular script called small seal script or *xiaozhuan*, consisting of about 12,000 characters, each the same size. This was used for stone inscriptions and also on seals, which were very important in China both for showing ownership and for approving official documents. Seals carved with the owner's name were made of many materials, including bronze, stone, horn and wood, and were impressed into clay and later into red ink paste before being stamped on to the document or painting. Another type of seal script is called large seal script or *dazhuan*.

In the Han dynasty (206 BC–AD 220), with the development of paper and silk, clerical script or *lishu* replaced seal script on most official documents. It has also been found on bamboo slips, which were strung together and rolled up like a scroll. Clerical script, ultimately derived from seal script, is characterized by considerable differences in stroke width and by a prominent diagonal stroke running to the bottom right of each character. A more fluent form of this script also developed, in which the characters are often run together or abbreviated. This is called draft or cursive script or *caoshu*.

In the period just after the Han dynasty a semi-cursive version, known as running script or *xingshu*, came into use, in which the continuous motion of the brush links what had previously been separate strokes. Sometimes individual strokes are eliminated altogether or condensed. The convenience of running script made it very popular and it is still the most common form in everyday use. Around the same time, in the post-Han period, there evolved the script that is the focus of this book. This was called standard script or *kaishu*. It is the most sophisticated of any form of Chinese script, combining distinct individual strokes to

Chinese scripts

rain

water

fish

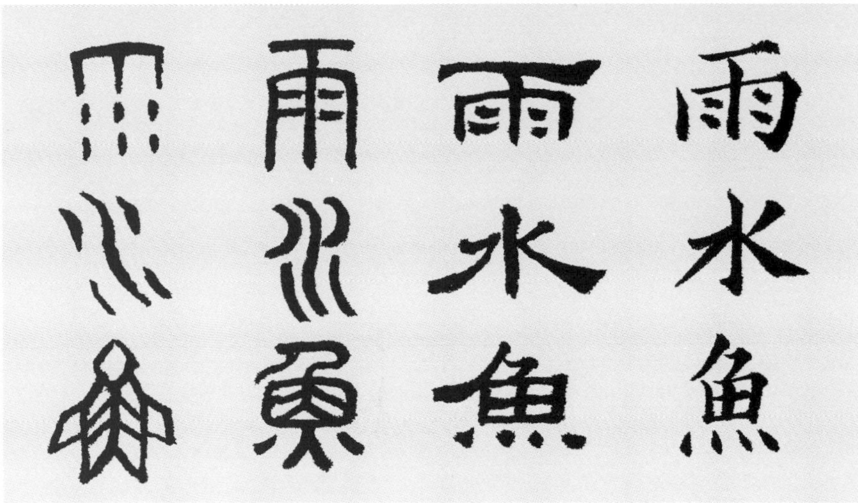

pictographic signs | seal script *zhuanshu* | clerical script *lishu* | standard script *kaishu*

make symmetrically balanced and clearly legible characters, as opposed to cursive and running scripts which can often be difficult to read.

The most famous Chinese calligrapher, Wang Xizhi (AD 303–61), was proficient in standard, running and cursive scripts. His son, Wang Xianzhi (344–88), was also a great calligrapher but less renowned. Many calligraphers have based their work on the style of Wang Xizhi, as the copying of old masters has always been encouraged in China. During the Tang dynasty, masters such as Quyang Xun (557–641), Yan Zhenqing (709–85) and Liu Gongquan (778–865) perfected standard script. The invention of woodblock printing at this time meant that *kaishu* became the preferred form for printed books. Later master calligraphers include the eccentric Mi Fu (1051–1107), Zhao Mengfu (1254–1322) and Dong Qichang (1555–1636). Zhao and Dong used calligraphic techniques in painting as well as painting effects in calligraphy, showing the close connection between the two. As both calligraphy and painting are done with the brush, the disciplined use of the brush in calligraphy was considered a prerequisite to the study of painting. In fact, calligraphy was always held in higher regard than painting, and good calligraphy was traditionally associated with moral rectitude.

Many, but not all, Chinese characters developed from simple pictograms such as a man or a horse. Each character is based on a square and is made up of one part which indicates the meaning of the word (the radical) and another part that sometimes gives an idea of the sound (the phonetic). In traditional Chinese dictionaries, the radical is located first and then the number of additional strokes is counted to locate the character and its meaning. Chinese script was originally written vertically and from right to left, but these days it can also be written horizontally and from left to right.

The development of simplified characters or *jiantizi* in 1956 in the People's Republic of China was aimed at helping ordinary people to read and understand by reducing the number of strokes in many characters and often introducing simpler replacements, with the same sound, for complicated parts of characters. In modern China many people still like to practise calligraphy, both in the traditional and more modern, avant-garde styles and using both traditional and simplified characters. The line of poetry on the back cover of this book is written in simplified characters, whereas the rest of the examples are in full traditional characters. Large handwritten posters in enormous characters (*dazibao*) played an important role in the Cultural Revolution from 1966–76. Chairman Mao was himself an accomplished calligrapher and his handwriting still adorns the title page of the *People's Daily* newspaper.

Jane Portal
Department of Asia, The British Museum

心正則筆正

‘Sincerity makes for correct brushwork’
Liu Gongquan (778–865)

The Four Treasures

Brush

Brushes vary hugely in size and in the type of hair, which can be quite stiff and dark such as wolf, weasel, badger or horse, or soft and white such as sheep or goat. Some brushes combine a stiff-haired centre, to provide a sharp tip, with a softer outside or belly to hold a quantity of ink.

For the beginner, a stiff-haired brush is easiest to control. As this was the type of brush used by the great calligraphers of the past, it is the most suitable for copying their work. The hair type or name of the brush is usually written vertically on the brush handle and beginners should ask for a 'large orchid bamboo' (*da lan zhu*) brush or a 'large white cloud' (*da bai yun*) brush. Check that the tip is sharp and that the belly is symmetrical and well rounded. For protection, the hairs of a new brush are held together by a water-soluble glue and sometimes a plastic or bamboo cap is placed over the tip. A new brush needs to be soaked for at least half an hour, and sometimes longer, in cold water to separate the hairs, and the protective cap should be discarded as replacing it can damage the opened hairs of the brush. The wet brush should be wiped to a point on a piece of cloth or tissue and left to dry flat or hanging from the loop at the end of the handle. When the brush is dry, shake it to separate the hairs and then store it, tip upwards, in a brushpot.

After use the brush should always be washed thoroughly in cold water–hot water may dissolve the glue holding the hairs in place. If ink is left to dry and harden on the brush hairs, the brush may be ruined.

Ink

Chinese ink is made from the soot of burnt pinewood, or oil smoke (lampblack), mixed with varying amounts of glue. The ink may be poured into moulds and dried to form inksticks, or it may be bottled as liquid. Bottled ink is fine for beginners, but there is something rather special about an inkstick and the calming ritual of grinding it on an inkstone before settling down to write.

Inksticks vary in quality and degree of decoration. In fact some inksticks are specially created as gifts or collector's pieces and are not actually intended for use. The creation of inksticks is an art form in itself. A beginner is reliant on advice, or price, but a good-quality inkstick should display certain qualities when in use. When wiped dry, the end that has been ground should be absolutely smooth and have a purplish sheen. The ground ink should exude a musky fragrance. Good-quality ink should dry waterproof on the paper. The damp end of the stick should always be dried after use to prevent cracking or chipping.

Inkstone

The necessary partner to the inkstick is the inkstone on which to grind the ink. As with inksticks, these can be exquisite objects in themselves, often irregularly shaped and embellished with carving. One end usually has a deeper hollow for collecting the ink.

To grind ink, a few drops of water should be squeezed on to the flat surface of the inkstone and the inkstick held perpendicular to the stone. After grinding with a slow clockwise motion for two or three minutes, enough ink should have run into the hollow of the stone. Of course, the thickness and darkness of the ink can be varied by the amount of water used and the length of time spent grinding. If the ink is too thick it will not flow over the paper; if it is too thin it will bleed and make blotchy lines. It is advisable to buy an inkstone with a cover, as this prevents the ink from evaporating if you pause for a while. At the end of a writing session the inkstone should be washed and dried, and fresh ink should be ground when you next prepare to write.

Paper

The most obvious characteristic of Chinese paper is its absorbency. This can be alarming for a beginner, as the slightest hesitation when writing will cause a blot.

The best paper for beginners has a smooth surface and is treated to prevent the ink spreading too quickly. Sometimes this paper is printed with squares, often subdivided for ease of copying (see page 26). Two suitable and relatively inexpensive types of paper for calligraphy are *mao bian* and *yuan shu*, both of which are brownish in colour and composed predominantly of bamboo fibres.

More experienced calligraphers work on *xuan* paper which is softer and more absorbent. Although most Chinese paper feels very thin, it is in fact stronger than it looks for it is made of long fibres. A piece of finished calligraphy will always have an additional piece of paper pasted to the back of it before the whole piece is mounted on silk. This process of 'backing' the paper makes the finished piece smoother and stronger and somehow gives the written characters a very crisp definition.

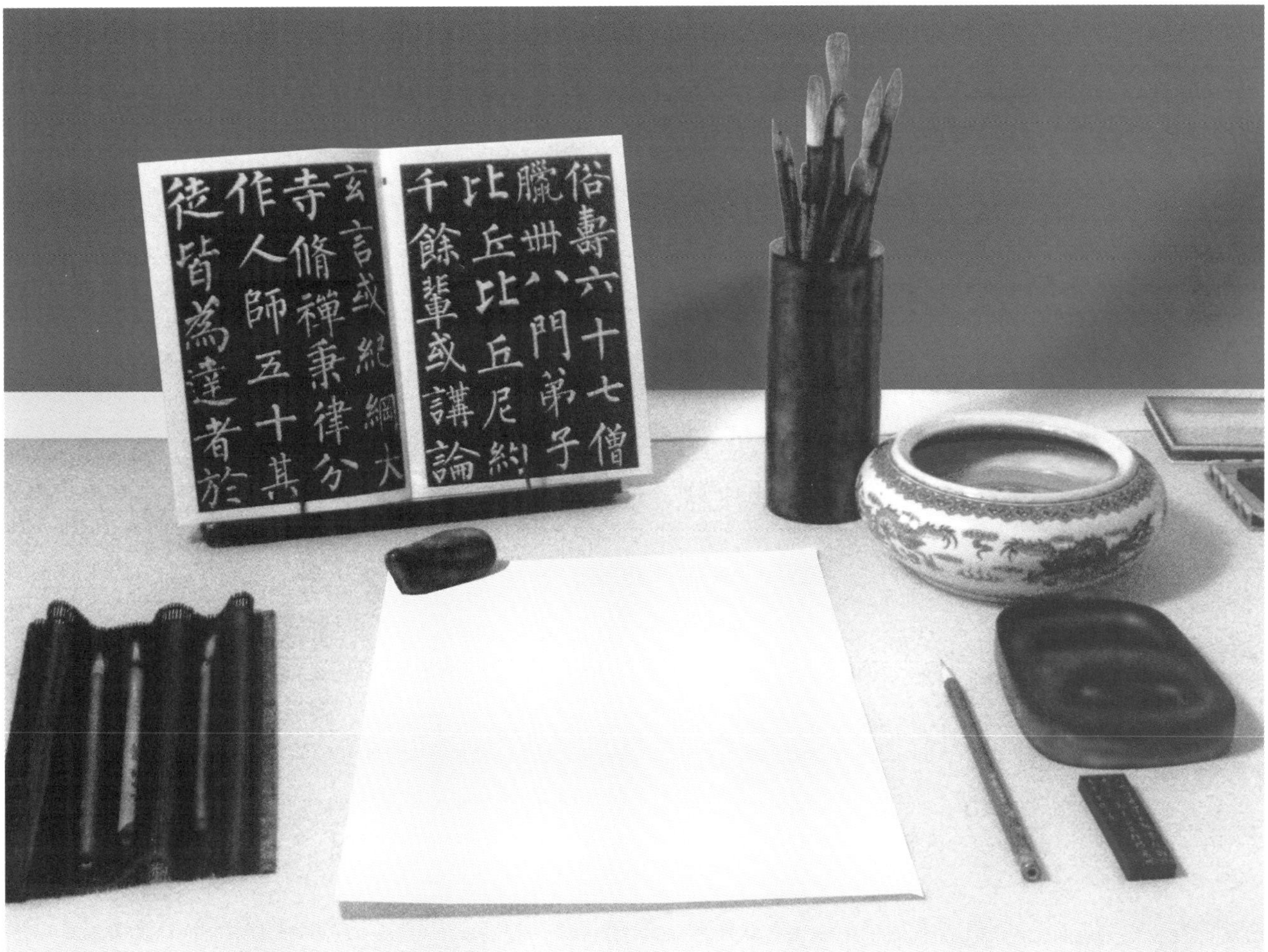

The writing table set for a right-handed calligrapher. If you are left handed, reverse the setting.

Setting up the table

The writing table pictured here shows the traditional tools and materials. These are of course ideal, but they can be expensive. For the beginner there are alternatives.

It is wise to invest in as good a brush as you can afford, of the type mentioned above. An inkstick and inkstone can wait. Bottled ink is fine for beginners. It is useful to have a shallow dish or saucer into which to pour a little ink.

The brush can easily be dipped in this and then excess ink wiped away, either on the edge of the dish or on a piece of cloth or tissue. The edge of the dish is also useful for stroking the brush to a point regularly while writing. If you are using an inkstick and stone, a Chinese ceramic waterdropper or a small squeezy bottle is handy for allowing just a few drops of water on to the stone. Suitable alternatives to Chinese paper are unprinted newspaper or even a printed newspaper itself!

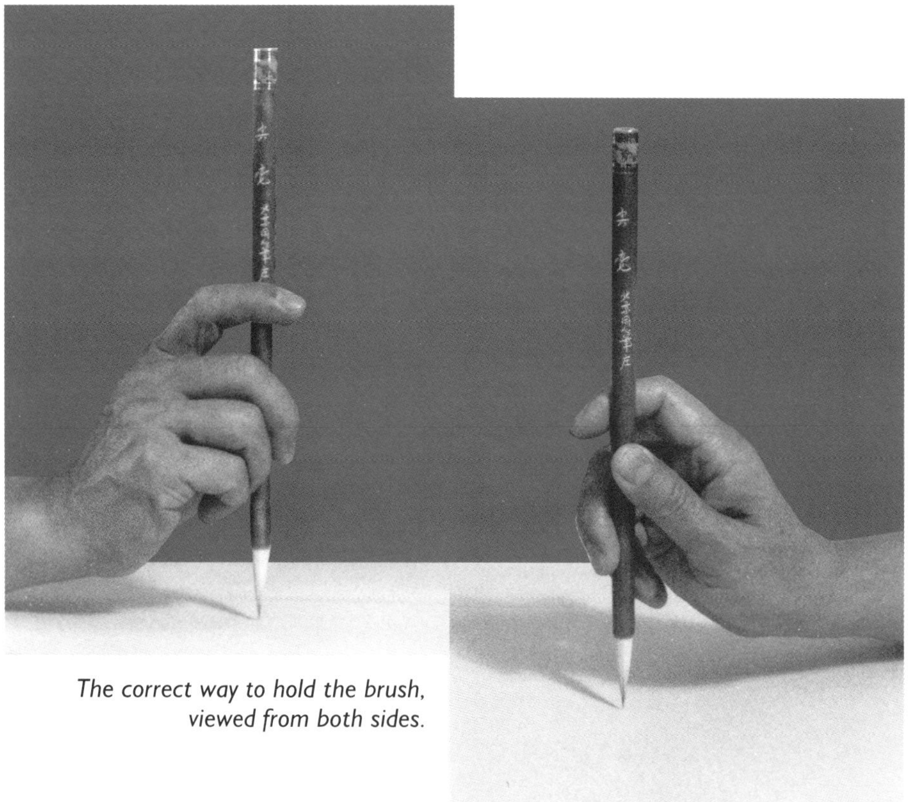

The correct way to hold the brush, viewed from both sides.

Taking up the brush

'Sincerity makes for correct brushwork'

These words, written by the great Tang calligrapher Liu Gongquan, are displayed on page 5 of this book. They illustrate how the term upright (*zheng*, second and fifth character) in both its physical and metaphorical sense, is central to the practice and theory of Chinese calligraphy.

The brush, as can be seen in the photograph, should be held upright, at right angles to the paper. One's body should also be upright: the back erect, with right angles at the hips and knees, and both feet firmly planted on the floor. A vertical axis should run through the body, and through a piece of writing: however varied the angles of many of the brushstrokes, the vertical stroke should remain vertical.

Holding the brush

In the standard brushhold shown (*zhi bi*), the brush is clasped firmly by the thumb and three fingers, with a hollow between them and the palm of the hand. The pinkie serves as support. The wrist may rest on the table or paper but should be free to move. With this hold the brush can be manoeuvred in any direction, thus allowing the 'way of the brush'. The brush should always remain vertical although it may be held at different points higher or lower on the shaft, depending on the size of the writing. Also, the angle of the wrist may change in much the same way as a violinist varies the angle of the bow.

Manoeuvring the brush

The next step is learning how to manoeuvre the ink-loaded brush on paper to create the desired forms. Experiment with simply moving the brush in the air, up and down, from side to side, round and round, and you will quickly realize the potential for movement. As well as directing the brush, you have to learn to exert varying degrees of pressure on the tip to create the contrast between thick and thin parts of a stroke. By pressing down you make a thicker mark, and by raising the brush a little you make a thinner stroke.

At the beginning you may find it difficult to think of all these points as you try to form a stroke. The absorbent paper leaves no time for hesitation! It is best to make a start and not allow yourself to be discouraged. Dip the dry brush into the ink and wipe off the excess, at the same time as turning the brush to maintain a sharp point (this must be repeated often while writing). A useful tip is not to overload the brush – the plump belly of the brush will hold enough ink for quite a few strokes.

The type of script you are about to learn is standard script (*kaishu*), which is the best one to start with as it provides the foundation for all other scripts. It is only by constantly looking and copying and practising that you will make progress. And by trying to make the strokes yourself you will quickly learn to appreciate the beauty of the strokes made by the great masters (see Gallery on pages 28–31).

The eight ways of the character *yong* (eternity)

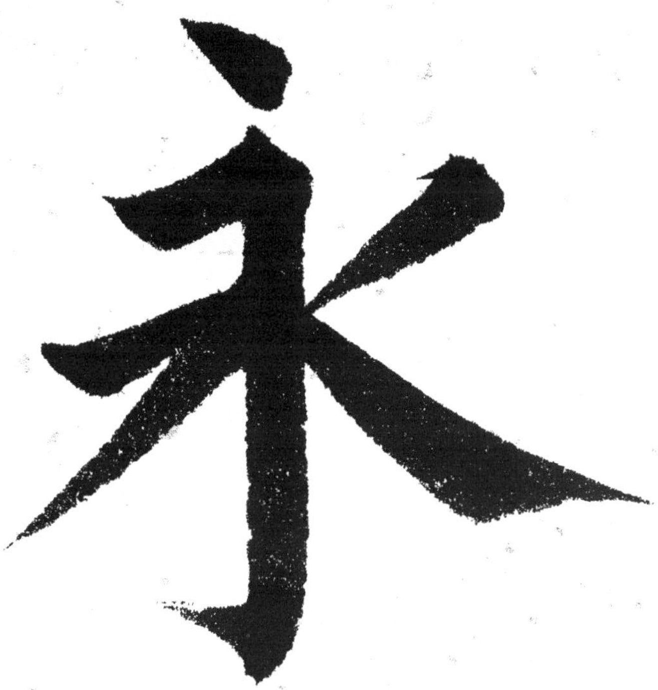

Modern Chinese characters have evolved over the ages, gradually undergoing a process of unification and standardization. However, there are still many disagreements as to the precise formation of many of them, which accounts for the ambiguities and contradictions to be found in books on calligraphy.

One of the earliest attempts to classify the strokes of standard script or *kaishu* was made by Wang Xizhi (303–61), who is considered by many to be the greatest calligrapher of all time. Wang Xizhi's teacher, Lady Wei, differentiated seventy-two types of stroke. Wang simplified her classification to eight strokes, all of which he identified within the character *yong* (eternity).

His book *The Eight Ways of the Character yong* has been much studied, and his theory can still form the basis of study for calligraphers today.

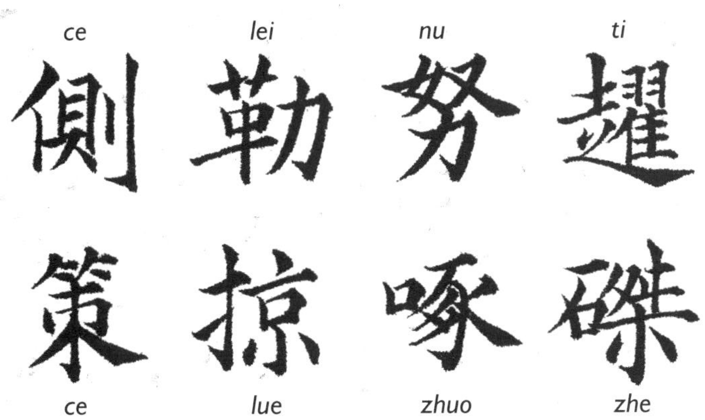

The eight ways

The original eight ways – or brush movements – necessary to create the character *yong* are:

1 ***ce*** (to shove)
2 ***lei*** (to rein in)
3 ***nu*** (to incise)
4 ***ti*** (to kick)
5 ***ce*** (to whip)
6 ***lue*** (to sweep)
7 ***zhuo*** (to peck)
8 ***zhe*** (to slash)

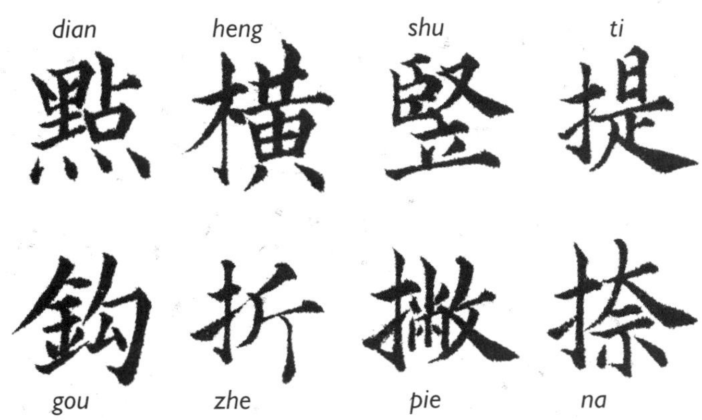

The eight strokes

The numerous brushstrokes in Chinese calligraphy can be condensed into eight basic strokes:

1 ***dian*** (dot)
2 ***heng*** (horizontal)
3 ***shu*** (vertical)
4 ***ti*** (lift)
5 ***gou*** (hook)
6 ***zhe*** (bend)
7 ***pie*** (left sweep)
8 ***na*** (right sweep)

Stroke One: Dot (*dian*)

點

The dot is the source of Chinese calligraphy, and all strokes can be said to come from it.

The top dot stroke begins with 'hiding the tip' and ends with the 'return of the tip'. Start by moving the tip of the brush upwards. Then press down towards the bottom right.

Next, rotate the handle of the brush very slightly, keeping the tip in the centre. Complete the dot by lifting the brush off the paper.

Top dot

字 character

高 high

Left dot

心 heart

雲 cloud

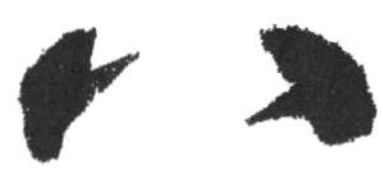

Left and right paired dots

Each of these strokes ends with the tip of the brush making a small point. The pair of dots is said to resemble two birds cocking their heads at each other.

炎 heat

光 bright

Stone dot

樂 happiness, music

玉 jade

Elongated dot

歌 song

不 not

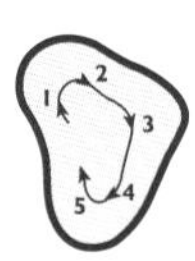

Top dot
brush movement

橫

The action made to create this stroke is said to be like reining in a horse.

To make a short horizontal, begin with an upward movement, then press down on the tip. Rotate the shaft anti-clockwise while lifting slightly, followed by a movement of the tip to the right. End the stroke with a small movement to the top right, then press down.

Finally rotate the brush clockwise and make a quick flick of the tip to the left to finish.

Short horizontal

正 upright

天 heaven

Long horizontal

筆 brush

安 safe

Left-pointed horizontal
Before touching the paper, move the brush to the left.

正 upright

非 not

Right-pointed horizontal
On completion of the stroke, lift the brush off the paper and make a slight movement to the left.

妙 amazing

朝 dawn

Right-hooked horizontal
The hook or flick at the end of this stroke is visible, yet merges in with the horizontal.

字 character

壽 longevity

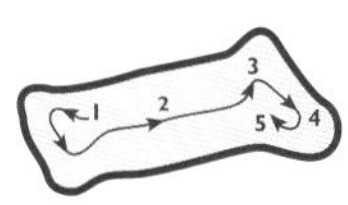

Short horizontal
brush movement

Stroke Three: Vertical (*shu*)

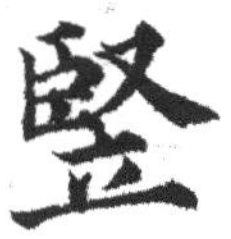

This is a powerful stroke, created by keeping the brush vertical and moving it slowly and deliberately, like drawing back an arrow before releasing it from the bow.

To make a straight vertical, begin by moving the tip of the brush upwards, followed by a downward pressure and a small clockwise rotation. Then move the brush straight down. Pause before rotating the tip clockwise to move the tip back up the stroke. Lift off.

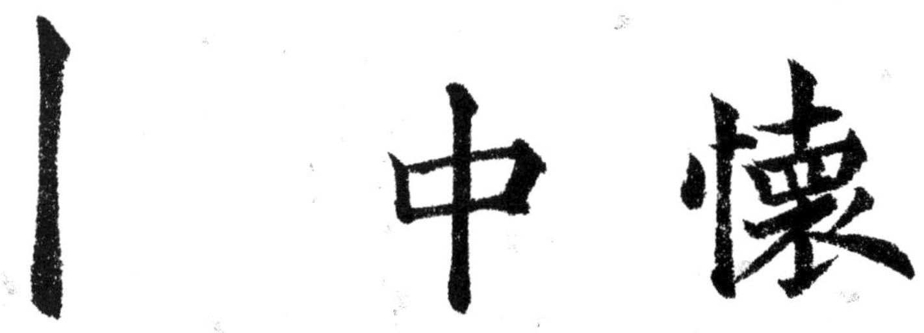

Straight vertical centre cherish

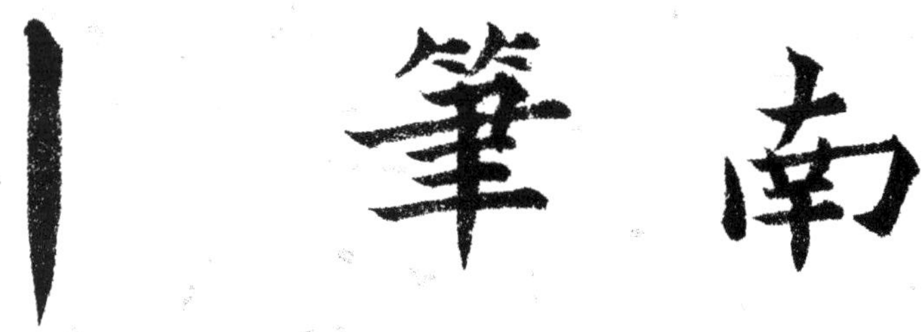

Sharp-bottomed vertical brush south

This stroke is made in much the same way as the straight vertical, except that the brush continues straight and is lifted off at the tip of the stroke.

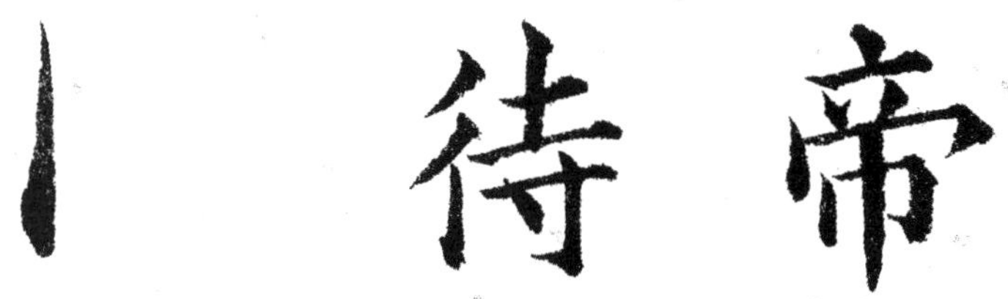

Sharp-headed vertical wait emperor

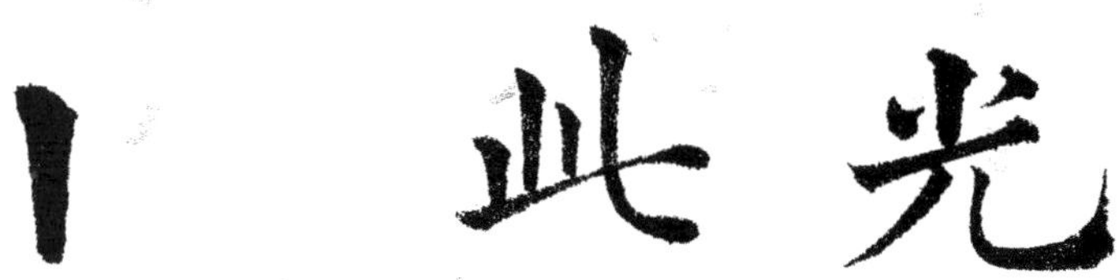

Short vertical (iron column) this bright

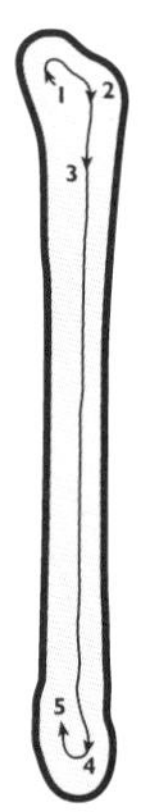

Straight vertical brush movement

Stroke Four: Lift (*ti*)

提

This is a triangular stroke. Each version points in a different direction, but each begins with heavy pressure and ends with a light lift off.

To make a squat lift, begin slowly and deliberately by pressing down directly over the tip, then rotate the brush ever so slightly in an anti-clockwise direction. When you are ready, flick off.

Leftward lift	我 me	身 body

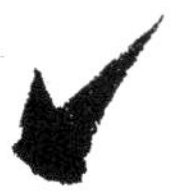

Squat lift	海 sea	冰 ice

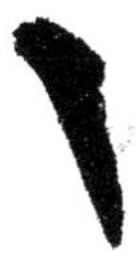

Top left (downward) lift	黃 yellow	昔 past

Top right (downward) lift	萬 ten thousand	並 together

Rightward (diagonal) lift	将 general	拒 refuse

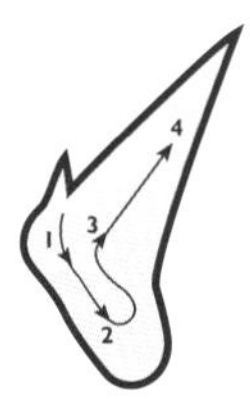

Squat lift
brush movement

Stroke Five: Hook (*gou*)

鈎

The brush movement for the centre hook is the same as for the straight vertical stroke until the end, when the tip of the brush is lifted off to the left.

The right-flicked hook is a combination of the straight vertical and the squat lift.

Centre hook — 東 east — 葉 leaf

Left-curving hook — 子 son — 學 study

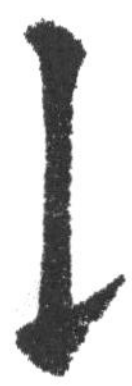

Right-flicked hook — 飲 drink — 能 able

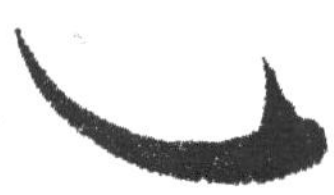

Shallow hook — 心 heart — 忘 forget

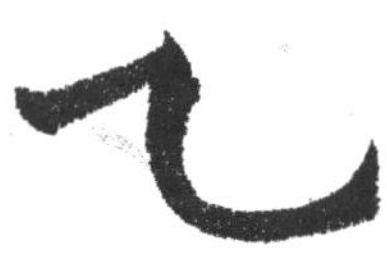

Two-armed hook (right bend hook) — 氣 air — 九 nine

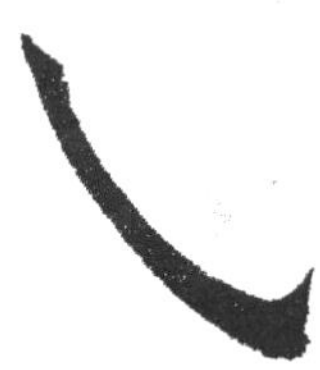

Long slanted hook — 紫 purple — 城 city

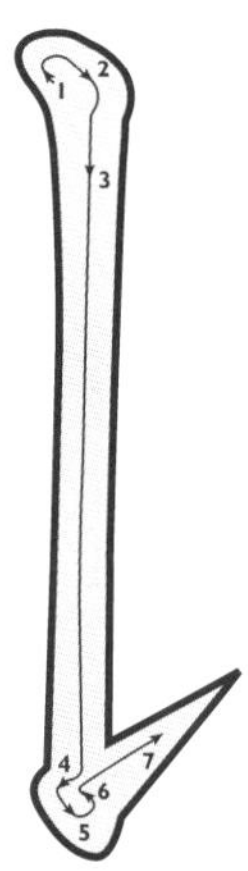

Right-flicked hook
brush movement

The bend may actually look like two or three strokes, but it is in fact only one, with a 'shoulder'.

折

When making a straight-armed bend, at the end of the first part of the stroke, gently raise the tip (without leaving the paper) and then press down with a slight rotation towards the direction of the next part of the stroke. Continue with the rest of the stroke.

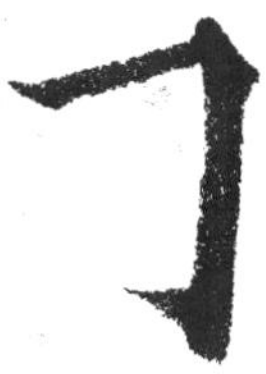

Straight-armed bend
This stroke is a combination of horizontal, vertical and hook.

則 then

國 country

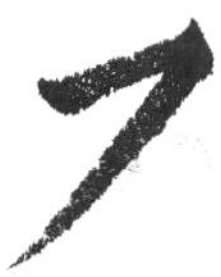

Left-slanted bend
This stroke combines the lift and left sweep.

永 eternity

泉 source

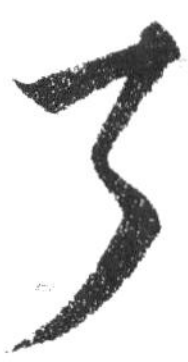

Three-corner (zig-zag) bend

及 and

道 way

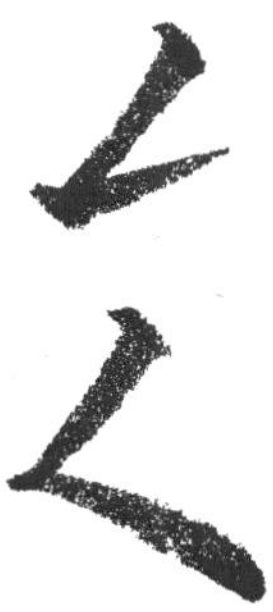

Right-slanted bends
These combine the left sweep and (top) the rightward lift and (bottom) the long dot.

玄 dark

安 safe

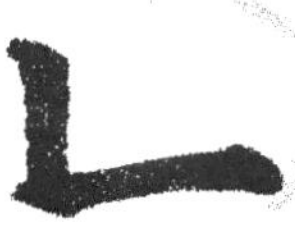

Elbow bend
In this stroke a vertical is connected to a horizontal.

北 north

世 century

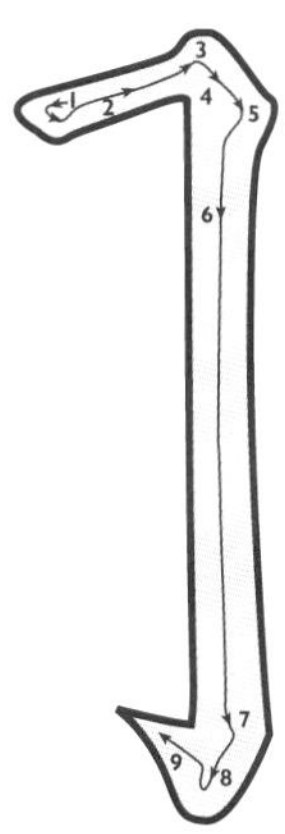

Straight-armed bend
brush movement

Stroke Seven: Left sweep (*pie*)

撇

This stroke is usually known as the knife or sword stroke.

The difference between the left sweep and the lift is that the sweep is slightly curved.

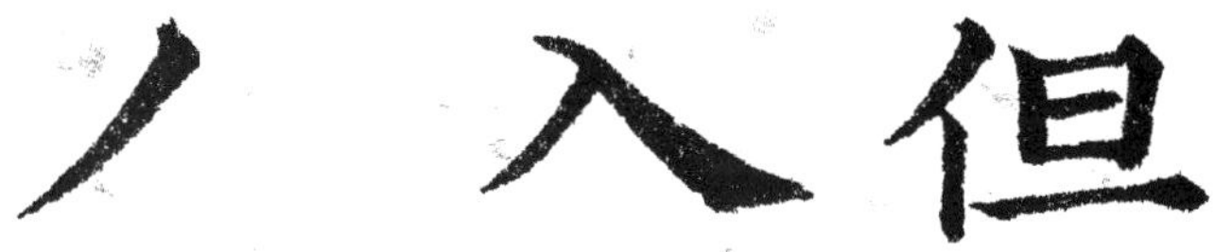

Short left sweep — enter — but

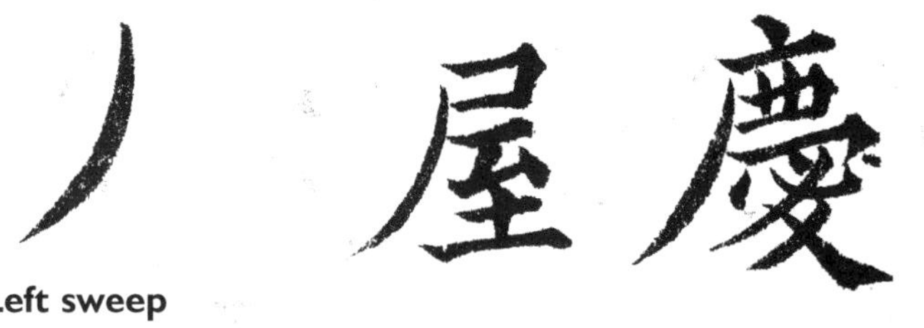

Left sweep
Often the middle section of this stroke is slightly thicker than the beginning and the end.

house — celebrate

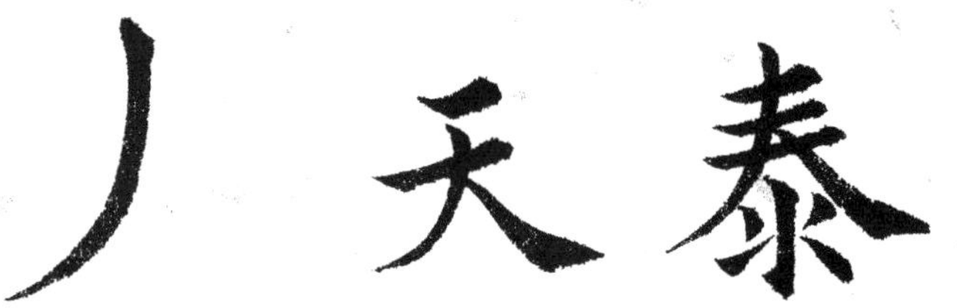

Central left sweep
This stroke begins like a vertical and then sweeps out to the left in a curve.

heaven — peace

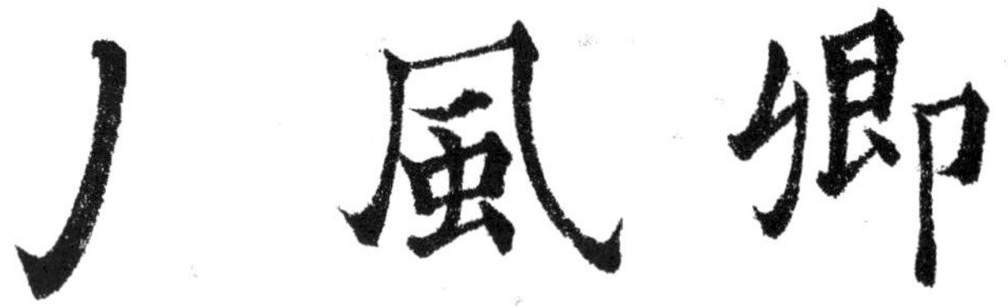

Hooked left sweep
This sweep is rather like a hook. Flick the tip upwards at the end of the stroke.

wind — official

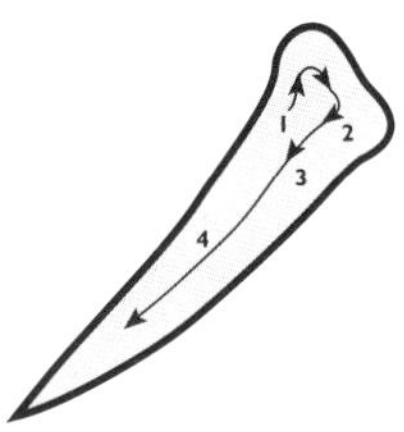

Short left sweep
brush movement

The right sweep can be long or short, thick or thin, but it always slopes and is fairly flat. It is made in a continuous movement with changes in pressure.

捺

The distinctive feature of the right sweep is that one edge of the stroke is almost flat while the opposite edge forms a triangle.

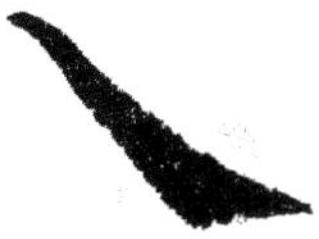

Deep right sweep
This stroke should be executed with confidence. The hand should not stick to the paper and the whole arm should be free to move.

大 large

夏 summer

Shallow right sweep
This stroke is not straight but like a wave. There is a saying: 'One wave, three curves'.

遠 distant

之 of

Reversed right sweep
This stroke looks similar to the elongated dot. In most cases the reversed right sweep can be used in place of the deep right sweep.

食 food

深 deep

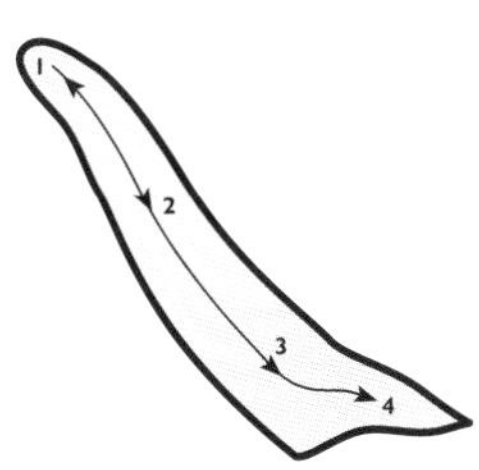

Deep right sweep
brush movement

Composition of characters

As soon as you feel comfortable with at least some of the individual brushstrokes you should move on to write characters, as this aspect of calligraphy is every bit as important as the formation of the strokes. Each stroke must be in the correct position and in the correct relationship to the other strokes forming the character. It is therefore essential to understand the different ways in which characters are composed.

1 Independent characters

These characters are each one independent unit and cannot be broken down into separate components. The area occupied by each character, which includes the space around it, is the same, although the number of strokes may vary. Characters composed of fewer strokes are usually written smaller to achieve balance over the whole page.

Whatever the size of the character, it is important to give it a stable centre.

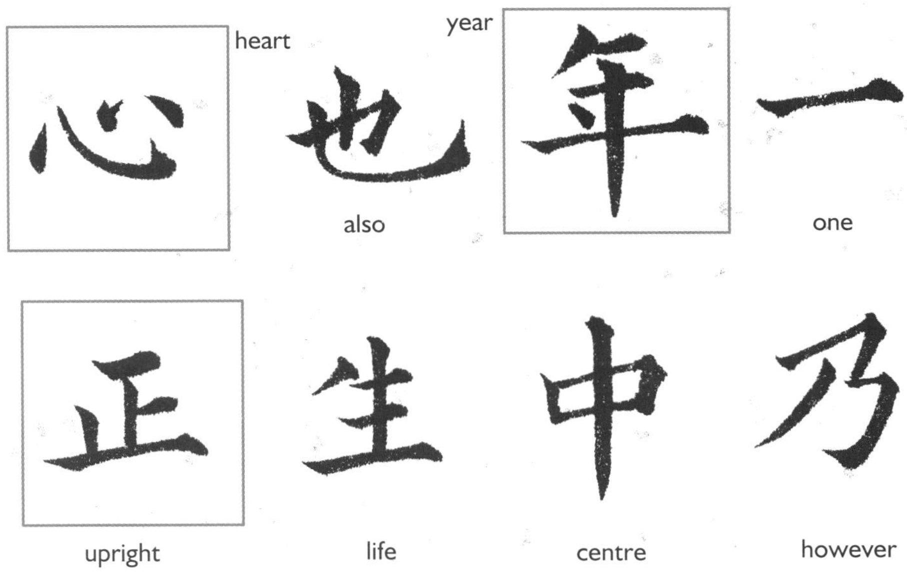

2 Characters divided vertically into two parts (left-right type)

This type of character is composed of two parts, left and right, one of which is the radical. For example, any character denoting a tree contains the radical for wood.

The two parts of the character should be balanced but need not be the same size.

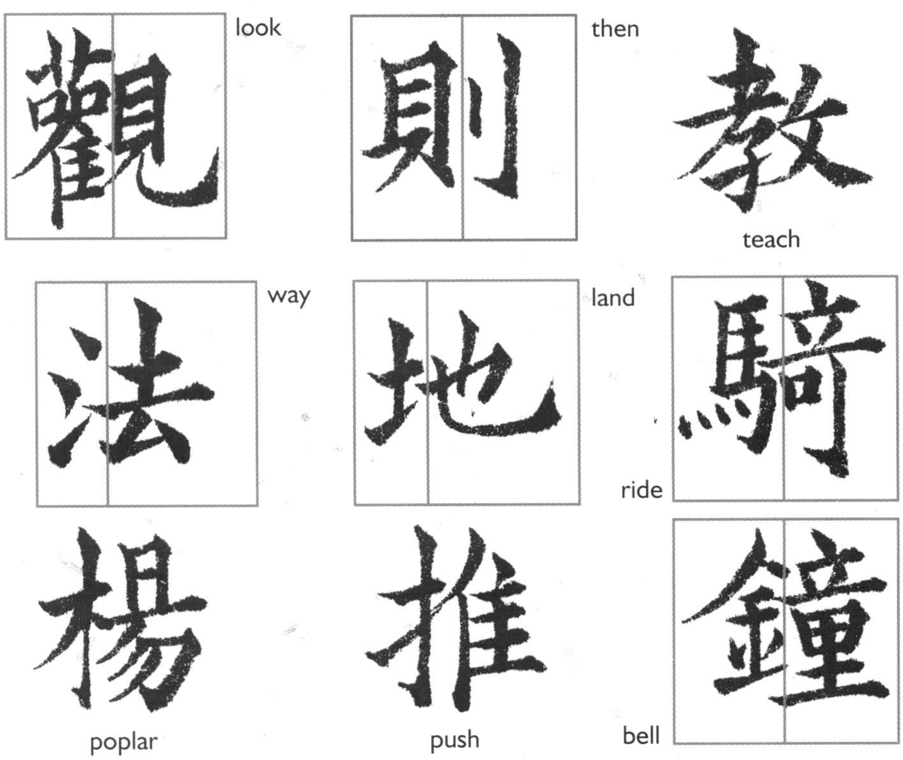

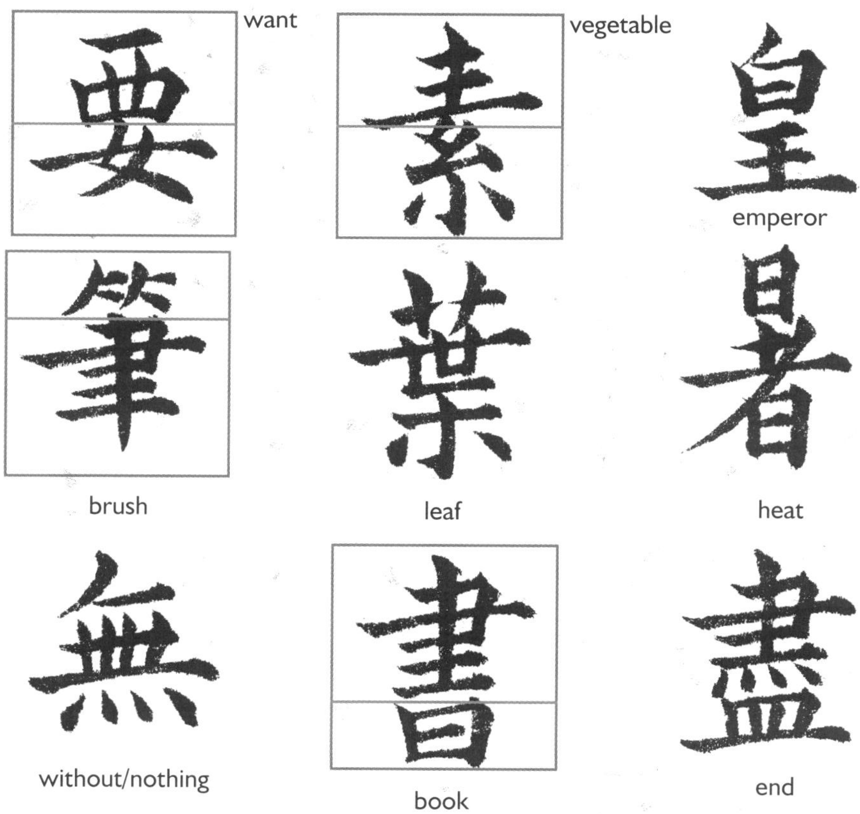

3 Characters divided horizontally into two parts (top-bottom type)

In characters of this type the radical is either at the top or at the bottom. For example, characters for all types of fruit have a grass radical at the top.

The distance between the horizontal strokes should be equal. If there are many strokes, the spaces should be smaller. Avoid making the character too tall.

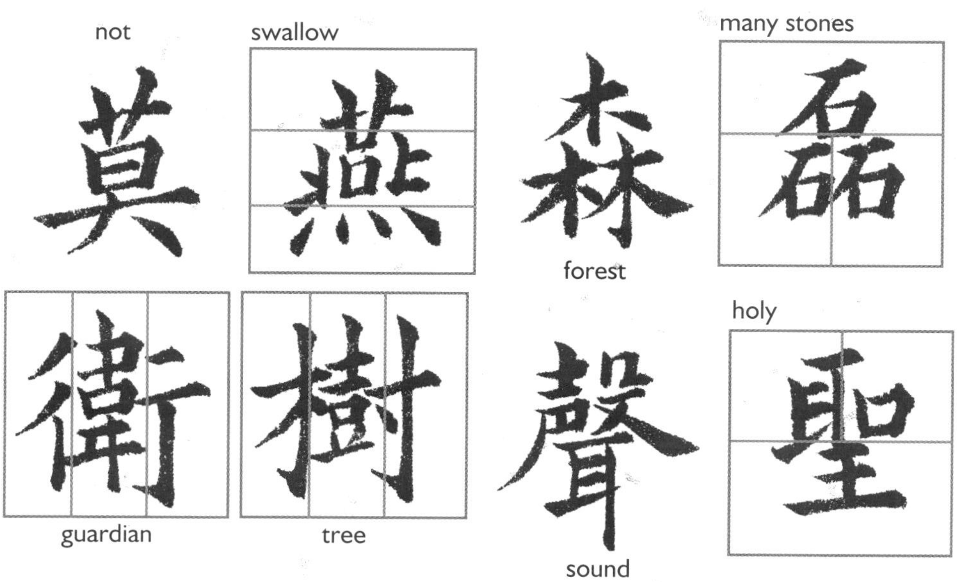

4 Three-part characters

The divisions in three-part characters may be vertical or horizontal, or a combination of both.

Care is needed to achieve stability and balance when forming these characters.

Composition of characters

5 Semi-enclosed characters

In characters of this type one part is enclosed by another, either at the bottom left, top left or top right, but never the bottom right.

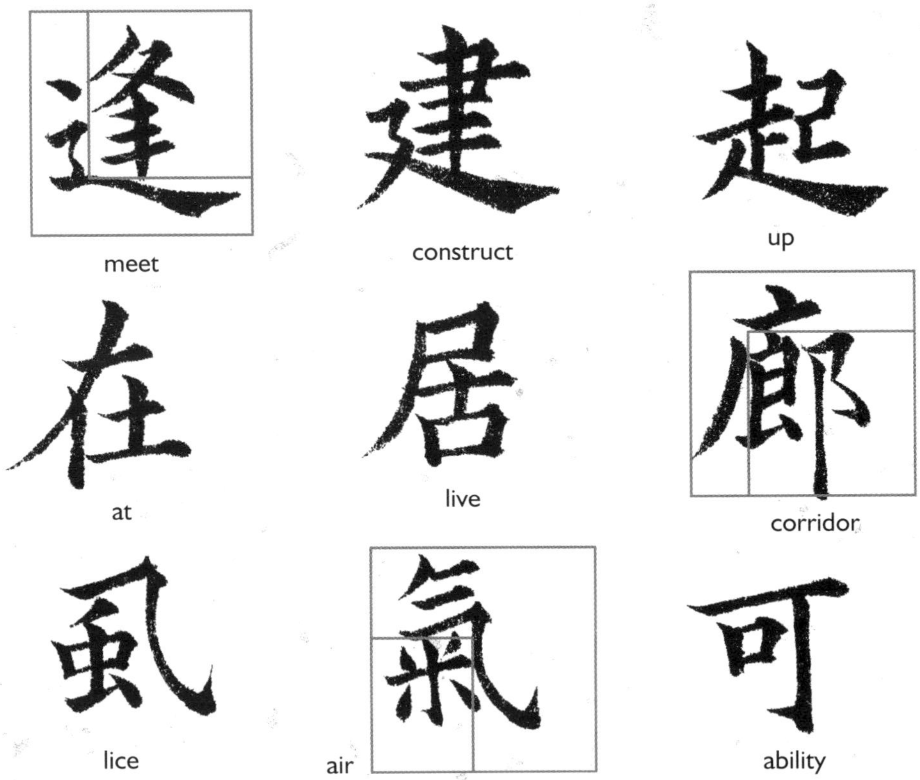

6 Three-quarters-enclosed characters

These characters are enclosed on three sides. Care should be taken to ensure that the proportions are in keeping with the number of strokes, so that no part is too large, too loose or too crowded.

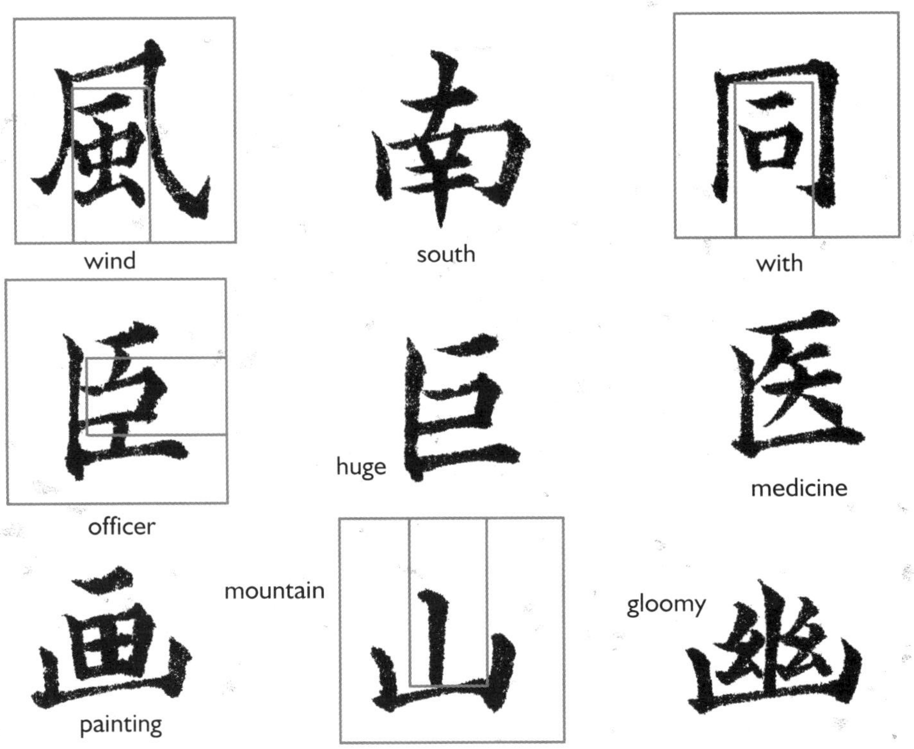

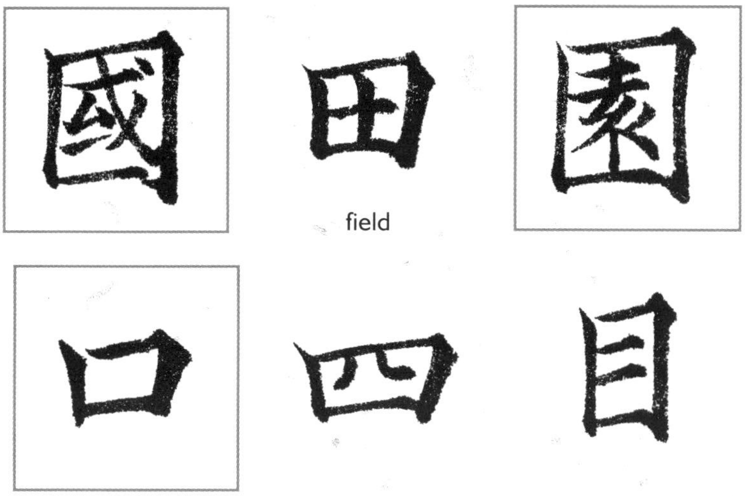

country 國 田 field 園 garden

口 mouth 四 four 目 eye

7 Fully enclosed characters

This type of character is completely enclosed as if by a wall, forming a square or a rectangle.

Take particular care with the size of such characters. More complex characters may be larger, with space within for all the strokes, creating a pleasing visual balance.

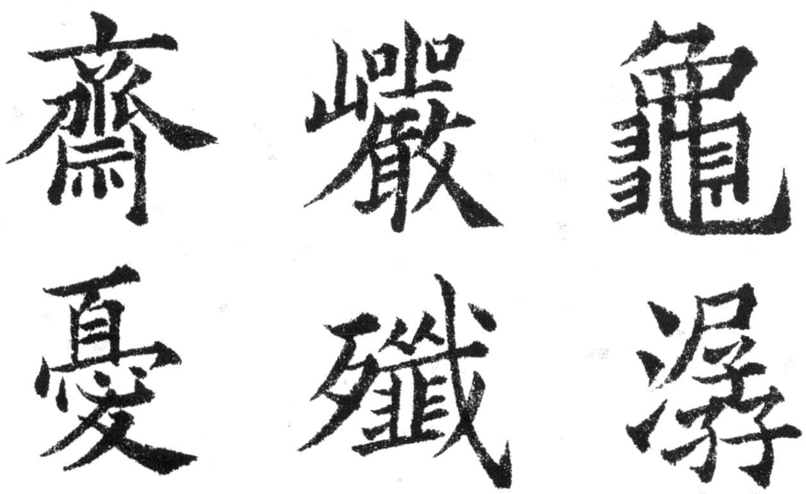

studio 齋 precipice 巖 turtle 龜

worry 憂 defeat 殲 babble 瀑

8 Complex characters with multiple divisions

These characters look extremely complicated, but once you have mastered the other seven basic categories you should find it easier to understand their composition.

In some cases, the more complex a character, the easier it is to arrange the individual components. Some of the most difficult characters to write well are those with the fewest strokes!

Sequence of strokes

Before the invention of paper, Chinese books were made of long vertical strips of bamboo or wood. When a person wrote, the left hand held the strip and the right hand the brush, and so the most natural way was to write from the top downwards. However, because of the many different ways of composing characters, they are not all written from top to bottom. There are a variety of sequences for writing characters, some of them impossible to explain logically.

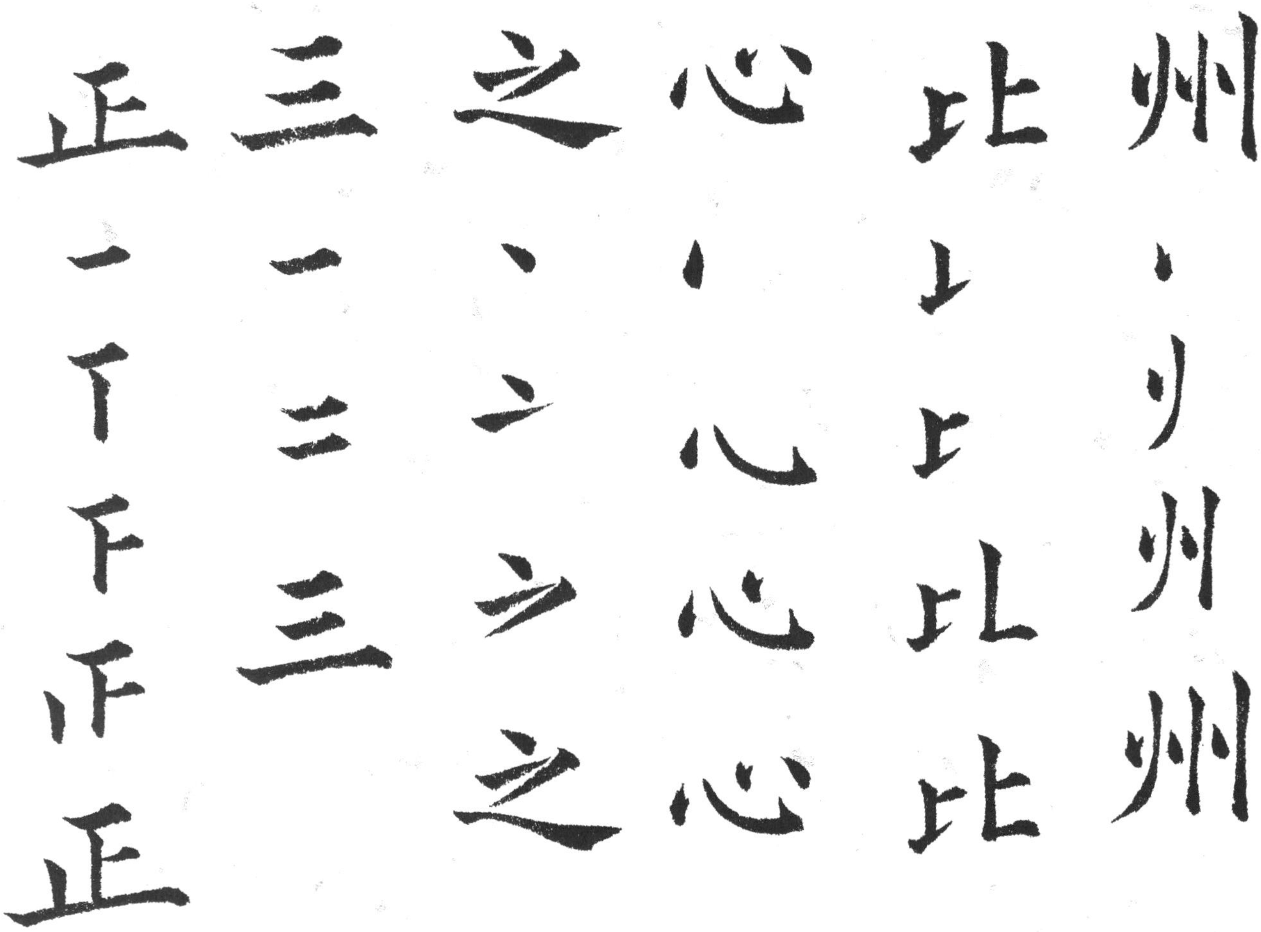

upright | three | of | heart | compare | continent

1 From top to bottom | **2 From left to right**

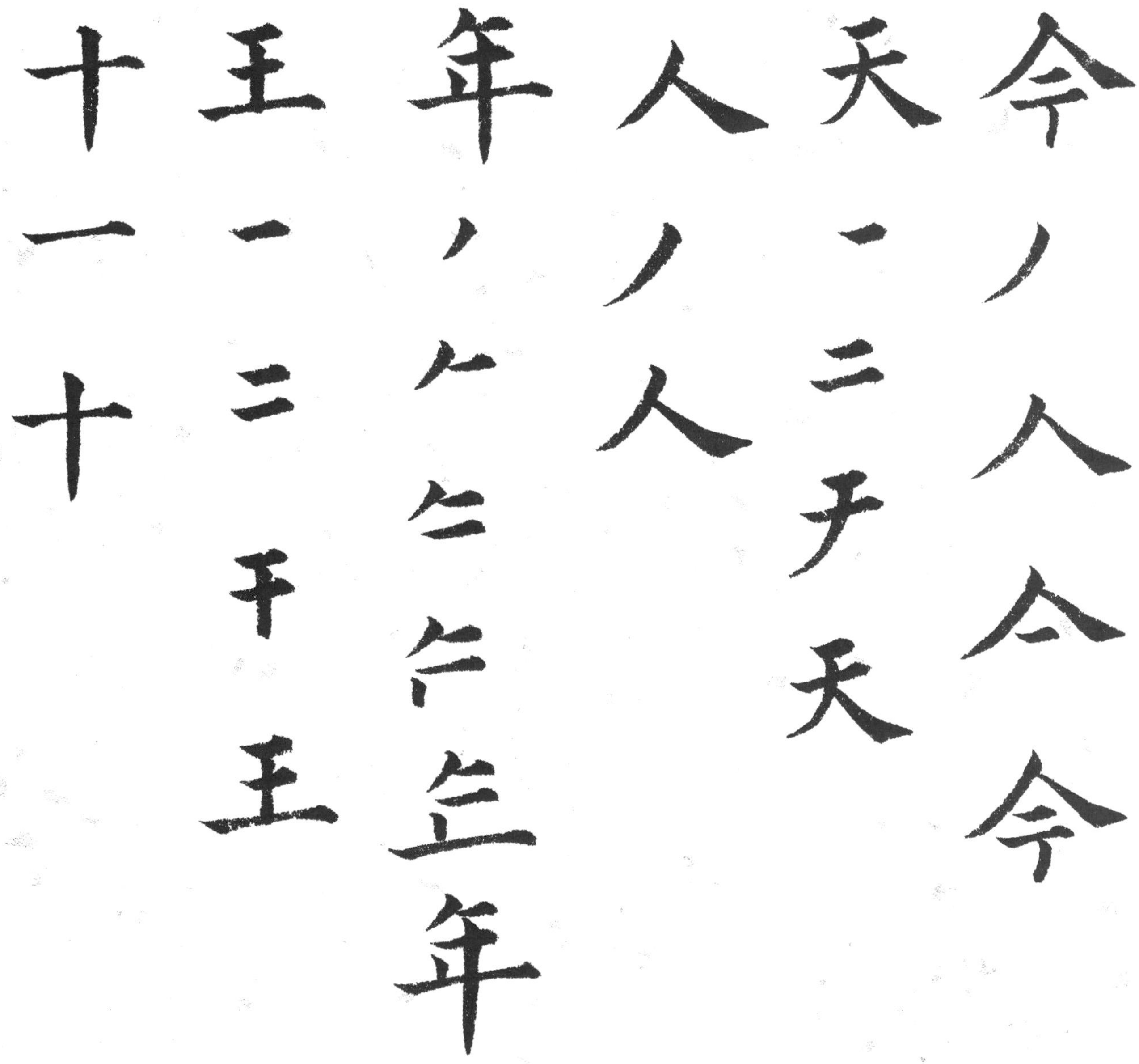

ten king year person heaven today

3 Horizontal then vertical

In characters where horizontal and vertical strokes cross each other, the horizontal stroke is usually made first. A horizontal stroke at the bottom of a character should be written last.

4 Left sweep then right

When a left and a right sweep occur as a pair, make the left one first.

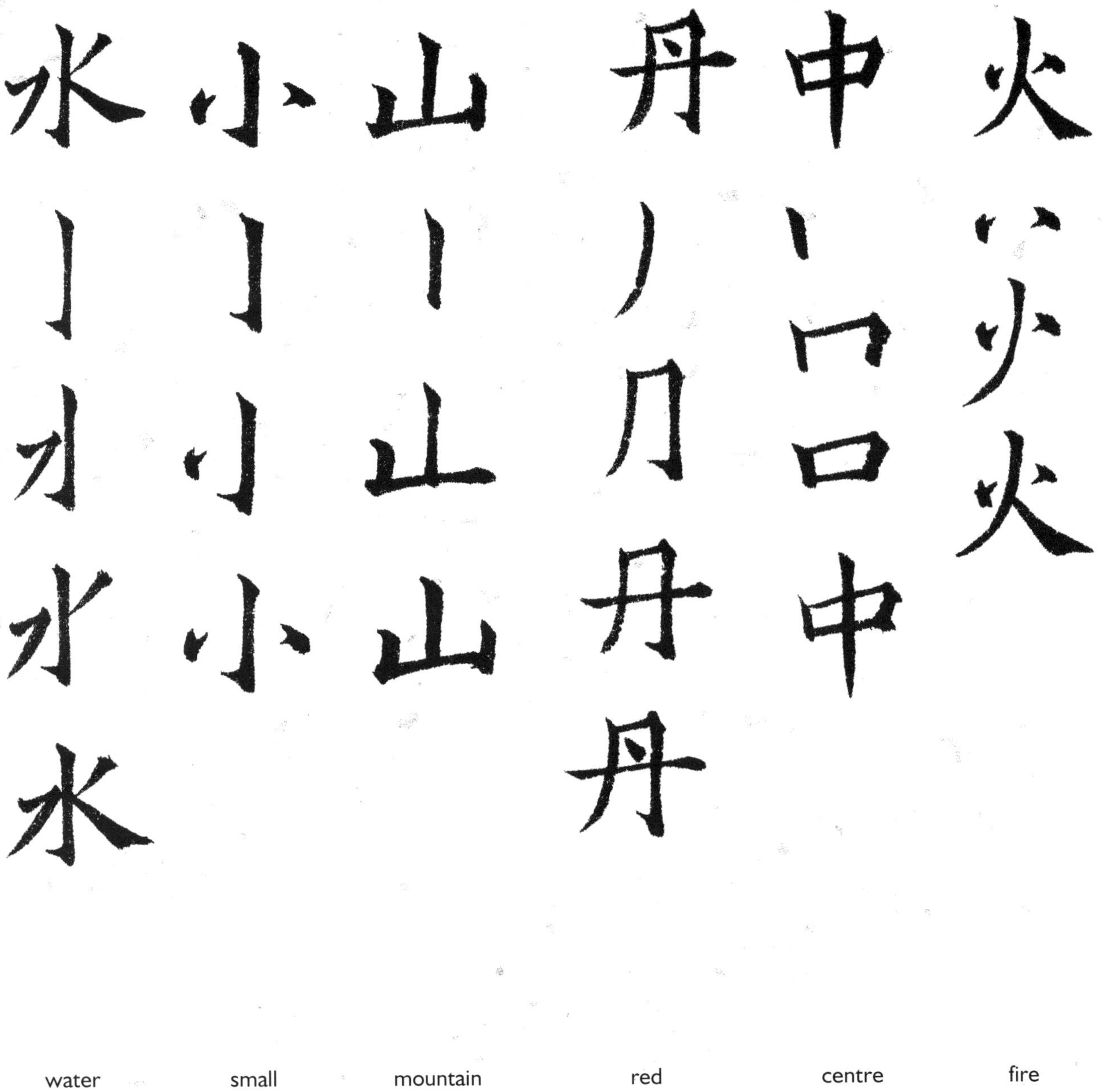

water small mountain red centre fire

5 From centre to sides

In some characters a major stroke in the centre forms the spine. This is always the first stroke.

6 From sides to centre

In some characters the centre part, whether large or small, is said to convey the spirit of the character. In such cases this part is made last.

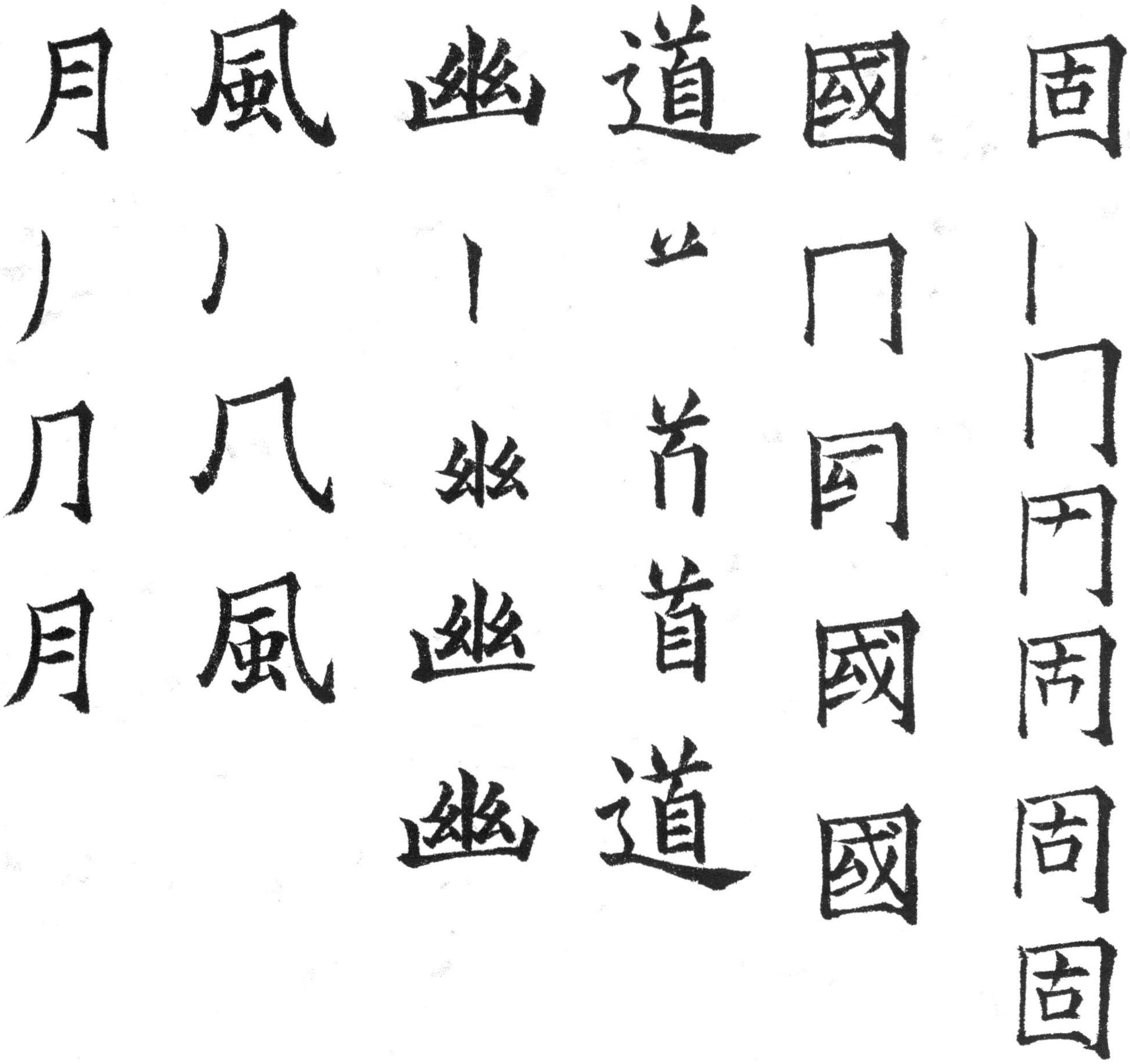

moon wind gloomy way country solid

7 From outside to inside

When the enclosure is above the rest of the character, the enclosure is made first.

8 From inside to outside

When the enclosure is below the rest of the character, the enclosure is made last.

9 Top three sides, then inside then final enclosure

This sequence of strokes occurs fairly frequently. The purest example is the character for mouth (see page 21), which is fully enclosed but empty.

Practice paper

Special ruled paper is produced for the practice of Chinese calligraphy, and this can help you to compose well-balanced characters. This paper comes in two versions: one is called the star or *mi* 米 (rice) pattern and the other is known as the nine-square or nine-palace pattern.

You can practise directly on to such paper or use it as a guide underneath your practice paper.

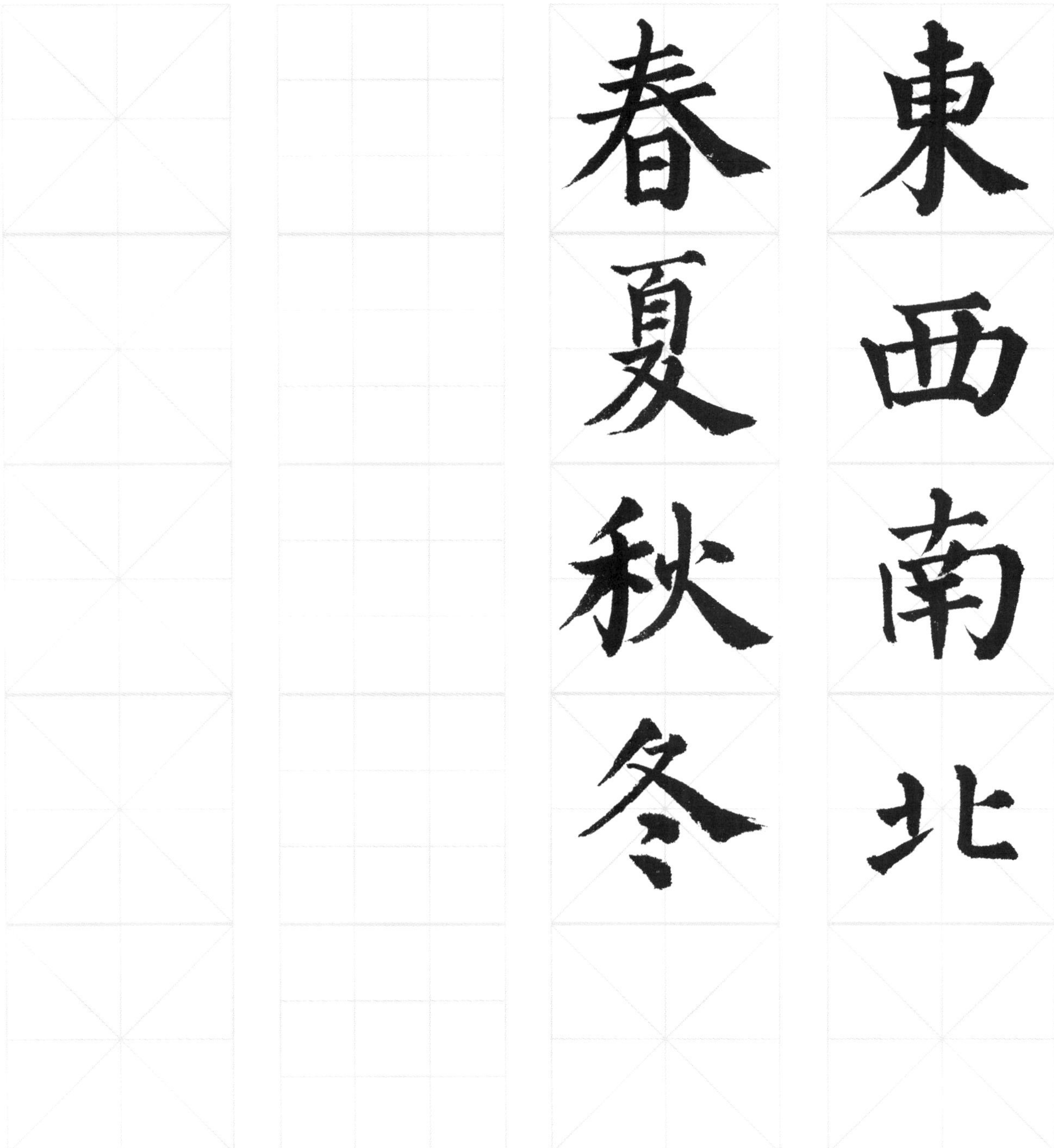

Star pattern

Nine-palace pattern

spring
summer
autumn
winter

east
west
south
north

中國書法

Chinese calligraphy

心正則筆正

Sincerity makes for correct brushwork

入木三分

Enter three *fen* deep into the wood (i.e. write with a powerful hand)

仁慈爲賢

The kindest is the wisest

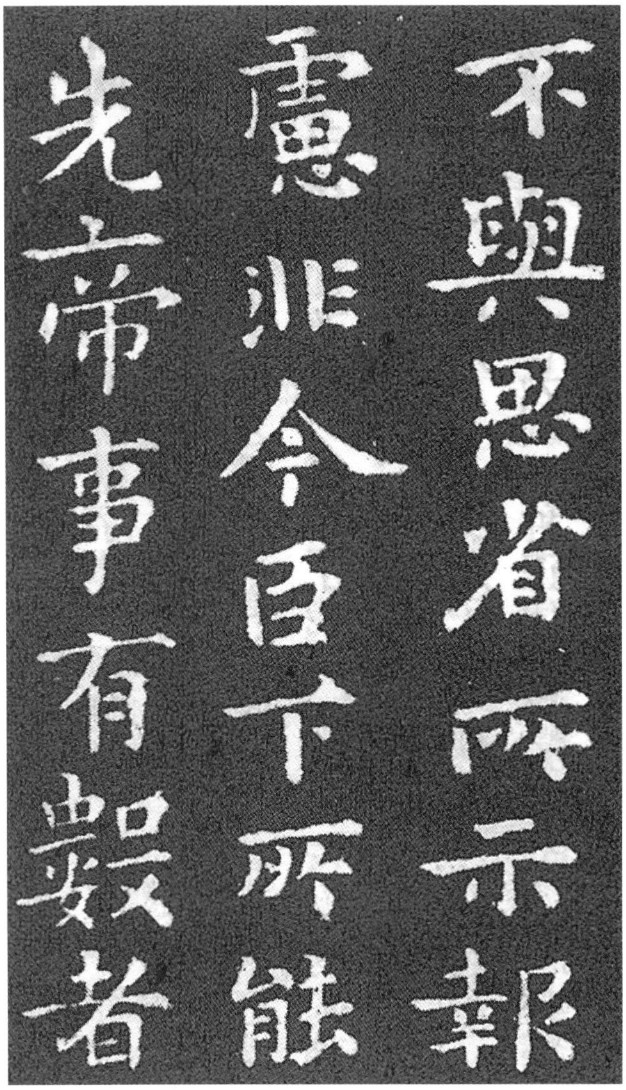

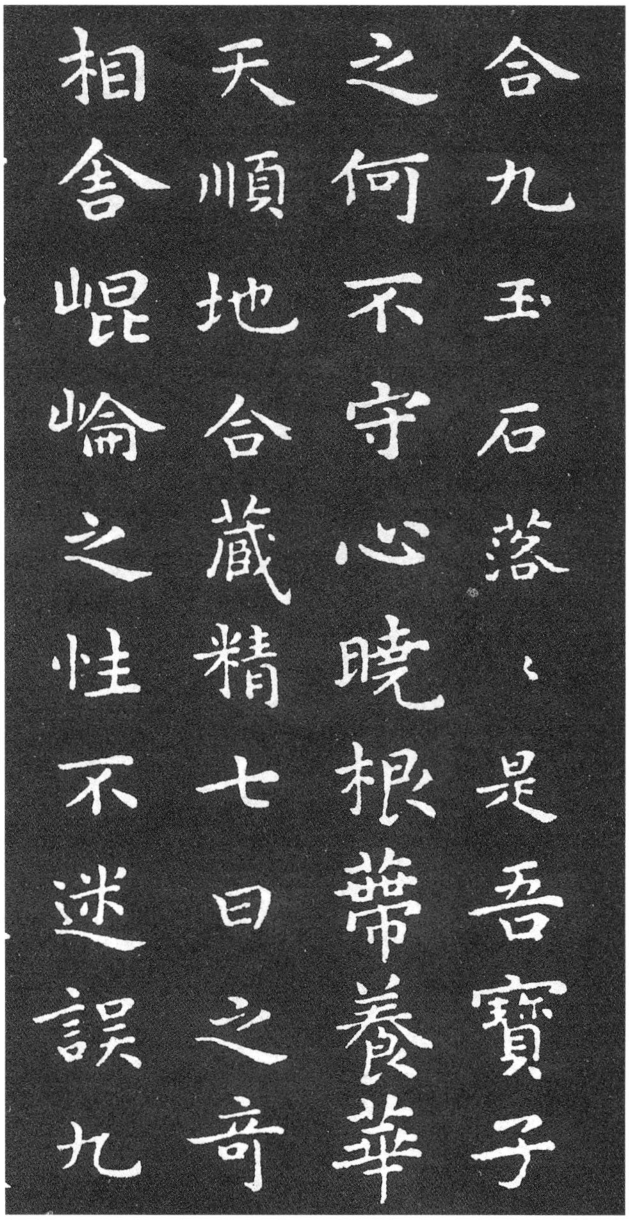

Zhong Yao (151–230) is known as the father of standard script. Tutor to the emperor Wei Mingdi, he researched calligraphy day and night. Even his bedclothes were torn because he scratched characters on them with his finger.

Wang Xizhi (303–61) is considered by many to be the greatest calligrapher of all time. His theories and his style of writing remain a powerful influence today.

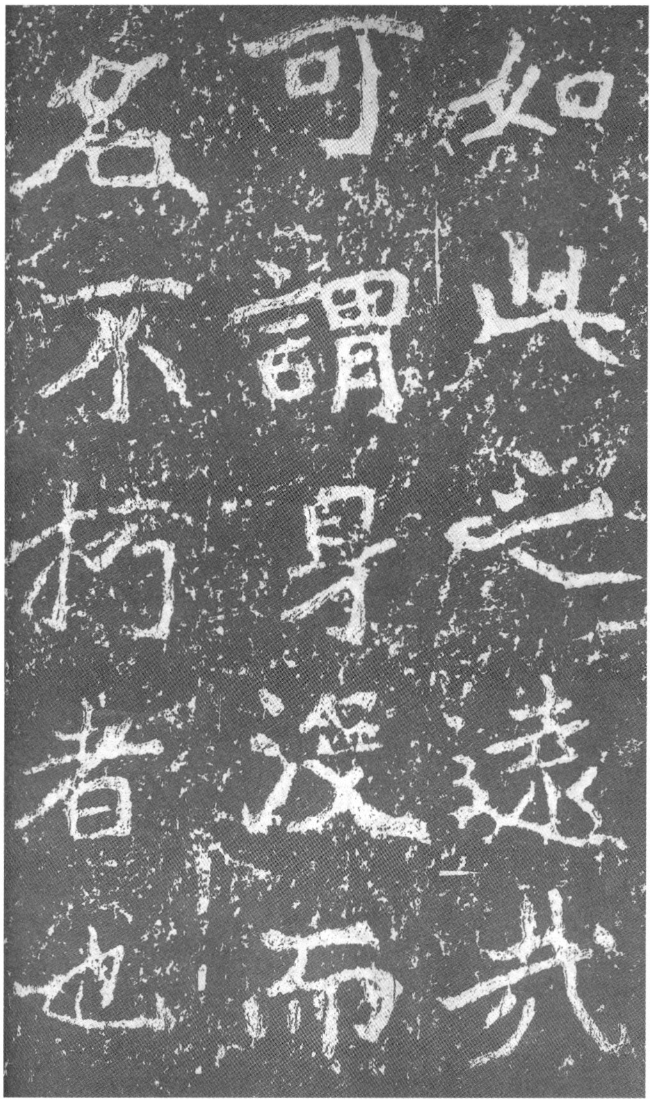

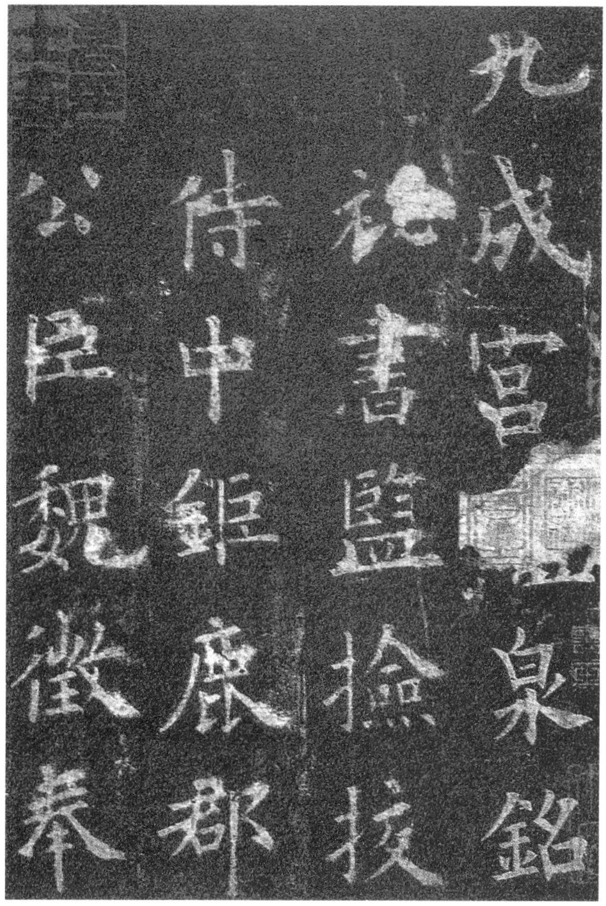

Zheng Daozhao (?–515) reveals in his writing the link between the official clerical script of the Han dynasty and standard script.

Ouyang Xun (557–641) is one of the great calligraphers of the early Tang dynasty. His standard script, known as the Ou hand, ranks among the four most important versions of the script.

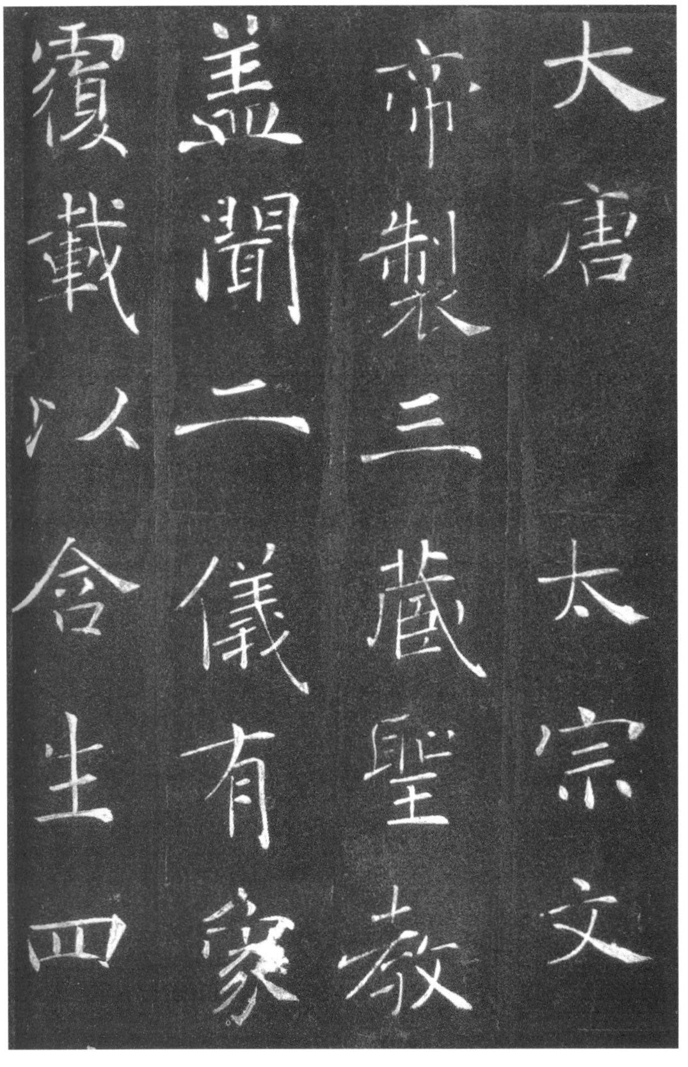

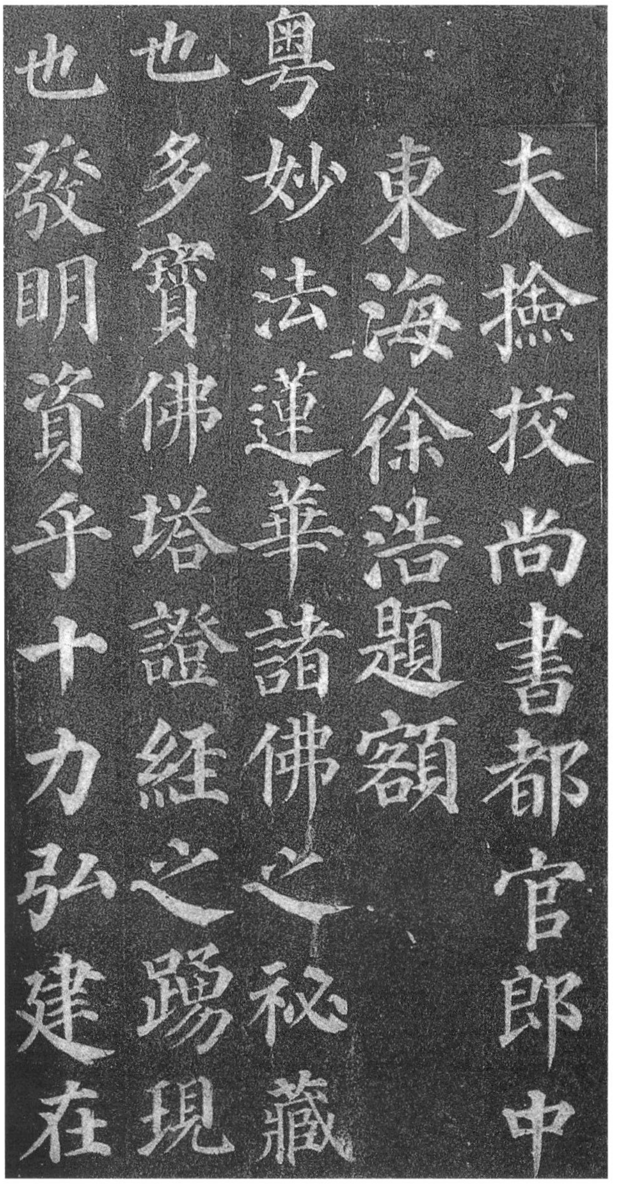

Chu Suiliang (596–658) is another early Tang dynasty calligrapher. His writing has the appearance of being delicate and sinuous, yet his characters have an inner strength and stability.

Yan Zhenqing (709–85) is one of the greatest calligraphers of the mid-Tang dynasty. His writing is upright, powerful and full of integrity. Known as the Yan hand, his is one of the four most important versions of standard script.

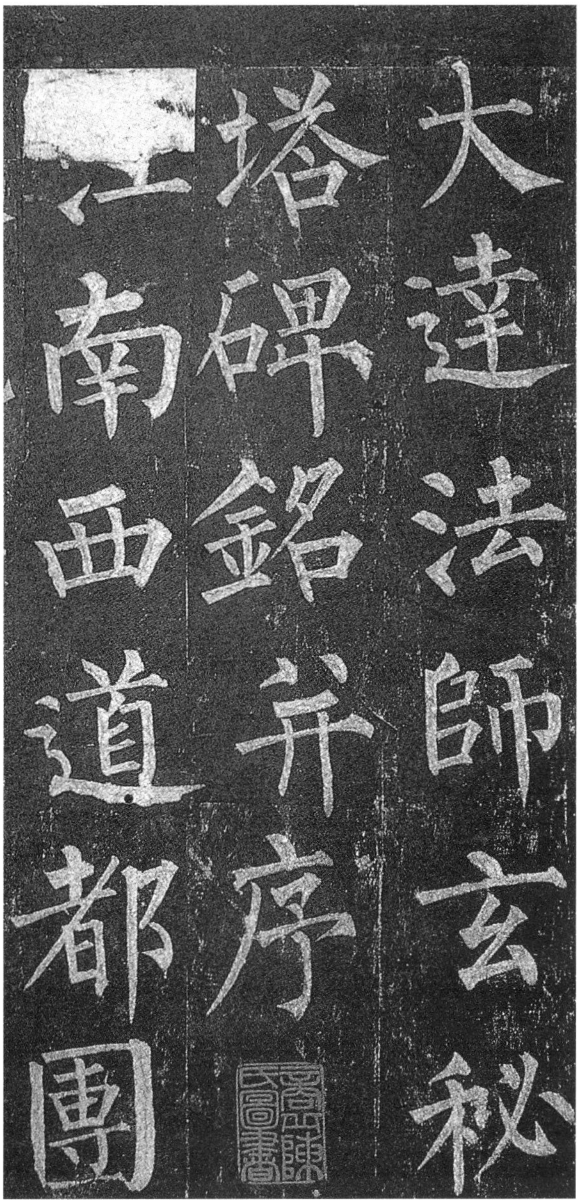

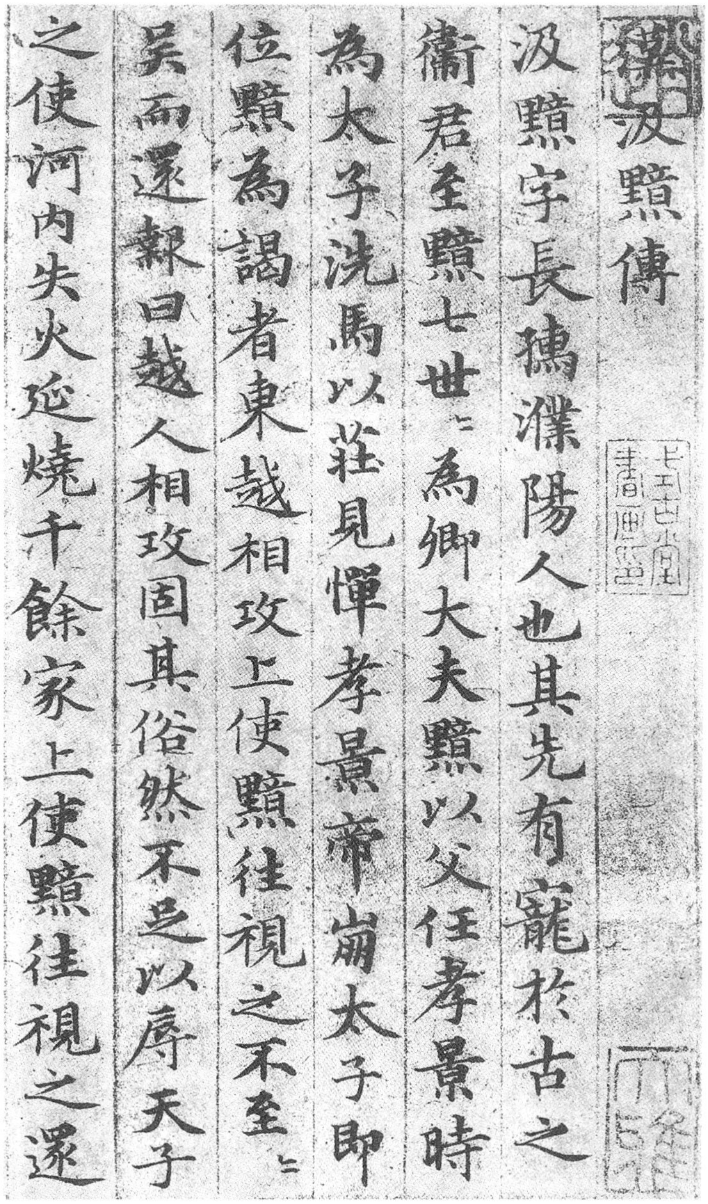

Liu Gongquan (778–865) is renowned for his powerful calligraphy which is said to have 'muscles of steel and bones of iron'. He wrote the famous words: 'Sincerity makes for correct brushwork'. The Liu hand is another of the four most important versions of standard script.

Zhao Mengfu (1254–1322) is the most famous calligrapher of the Yuan dynasty. The Zhao hand is the latest of the four important versions of standard script and one of the most popular styles in use today.

Bibliography

Practical guides

Chiang Yee, *Chinese Calligraphy: An Introduction to its Aesthetic and Technique*.
London: Methuen and Co Ltd 1938

Dahlen, Martha, Grace Ho and Ho Siu Kei, *Brush with Life: Writing Chinese Words of Virtue and Celebration*.
Hong Kong: United Century Book Services Ltd 2002

Kwo Da-Wei, *Chinese Brushwork in Calligraphy and Painting*.
London: Dover 1981

Liu Puqing, *Standard Modern Chinese Calligraphy (Kaishu biaozhun zitie)*.
Beijing: Beijing Press 1979

Qu Lei Lei, *The Simple Art of Chinese Calligraphy*.
London: Cico Books 2002

History and theory

Barrass, Gordon S., *The Art of Calligraphy in Modern China*.
London: The British Museum Press 2002

Billeter, Jean François, *The Chinese Art of Writing*.
New York: Skira/Rizzoli 1990

Fu Shen, *Traces of the Brush: Studies in Chinese Calligraphy*.
Yale University Press 1977

Lin Hongyuan, *Great Dictionary of Chinese Calligraphy (Zhongguo shufa dazidian)*.
Beijing: Guanghua Press 1980

Moore, Oliver, *Reading the Past: Chinese*.
London: The British Museum Press 2000

Sun Xiaoyun, *The Way of Chinese Calligraphy (Shufa youfa)*.
Beijing: Knowledge Press 2003

Yang Zaichun, *Handbook of Chinese Calligraphy (Zhongguo shufa gongju shouce)*.
Beijing: The Physical Education Press 1987

Zhang Yiguo, *Brushed Voices: Calligraphy in Contemporary China*.
Columbia University 1998

E.T.
THE EXTRA-TERRESTRIAL

DISCOVERS The Solar System

Ian Graham

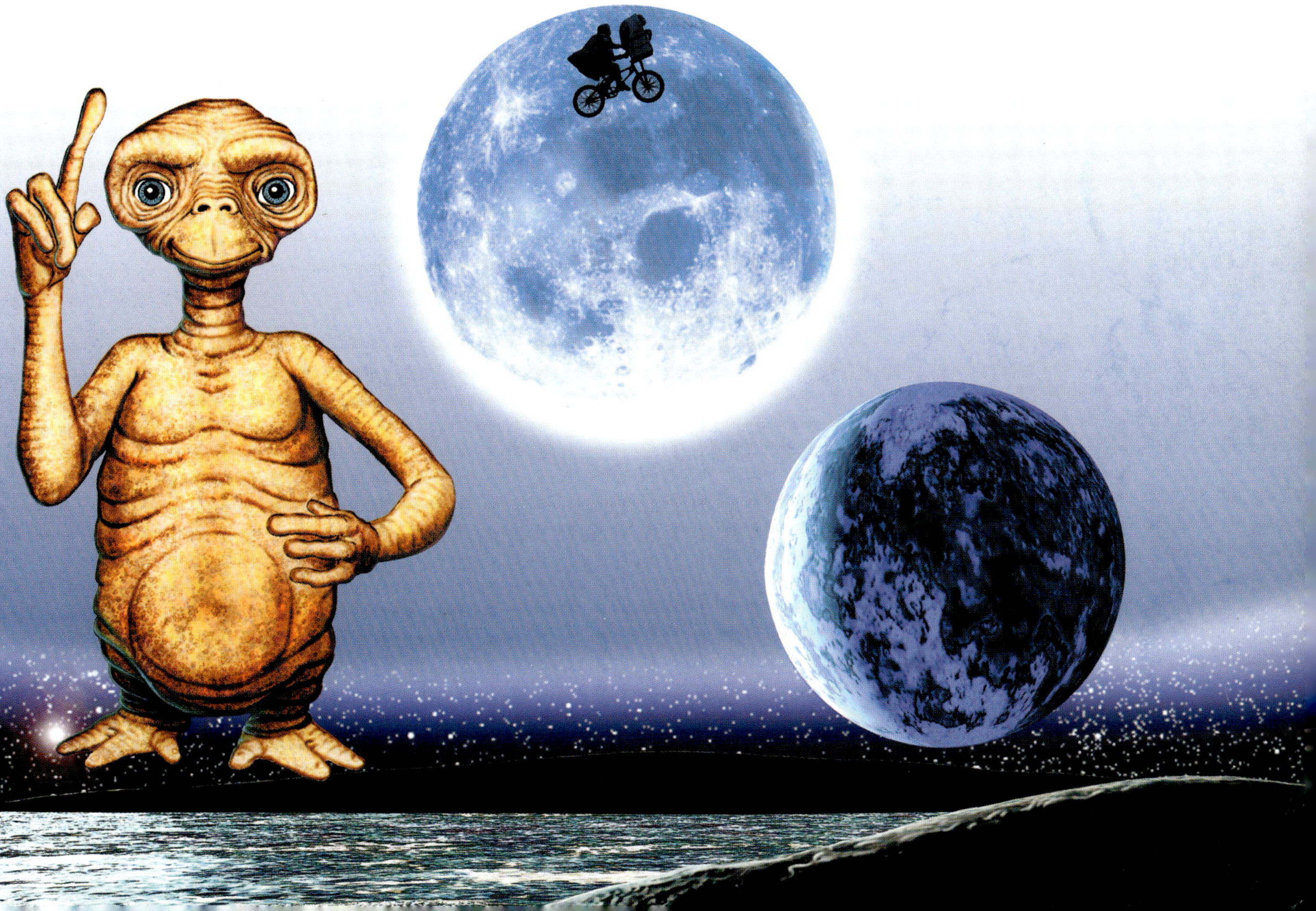

KINGFISHER/UNIVERSAL
Kingfisher Publications Plc
New Penderel House
283-288 High Holborn
London WC1V 7HZ
www.kingfisherpub.com

First published by Kingfisher Publications Plc in 2002

10 9 8 7 6 5 4 3 2 1

1TR/1201/TWP/MAR(MAR)/130SINAR

A CIP catalogue for this book is available from the British Library.

ISBN 0 7534 0732 9

Printed in Singapore

Author: Ian Graham
Project Manager: Belinda Weber
Editor: Christine Hatt
Art Editor: Eljay Yildirim
Designer: Andrew Nash
DTP Manager: Nicky Studdart
Production Controller: Debbie Otter, Kelly Johnson

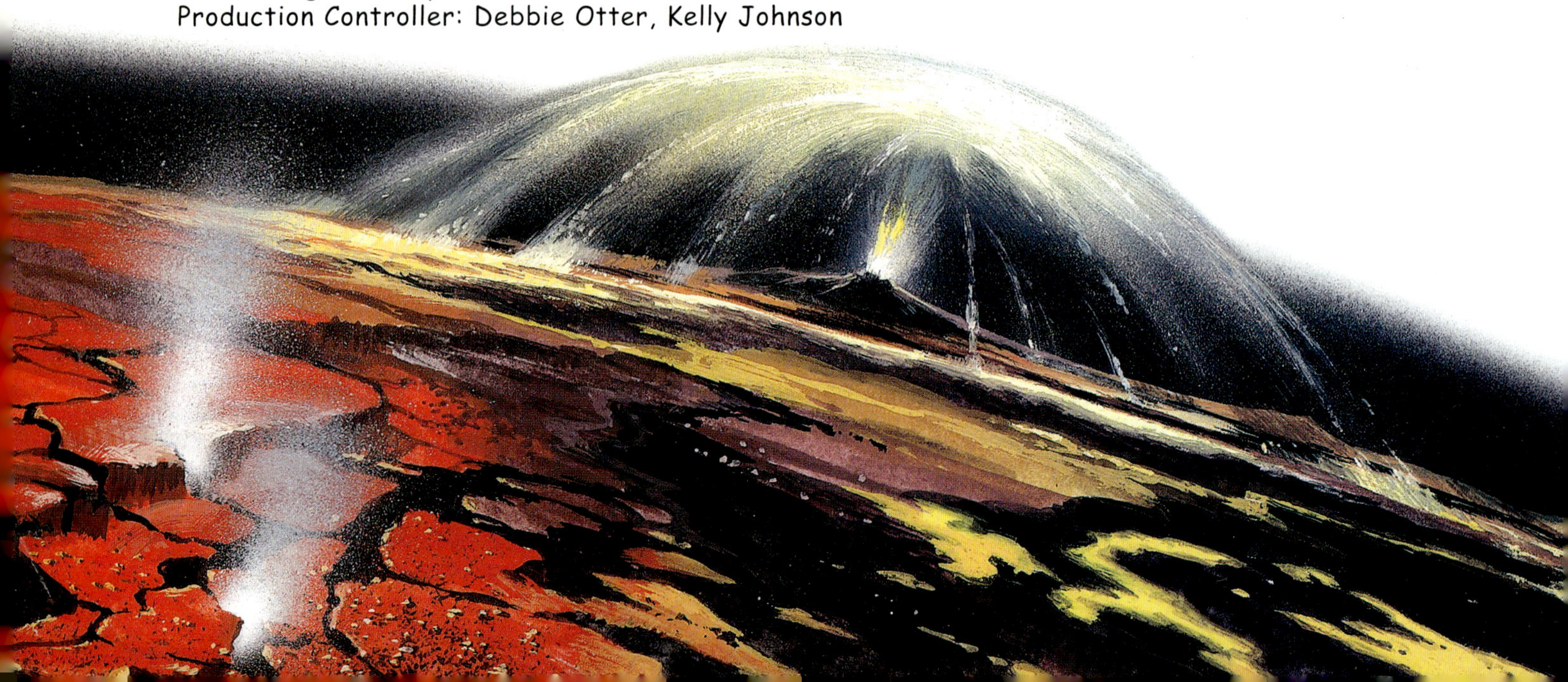

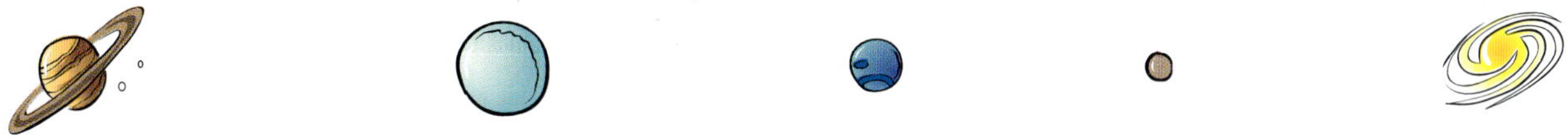

Contents

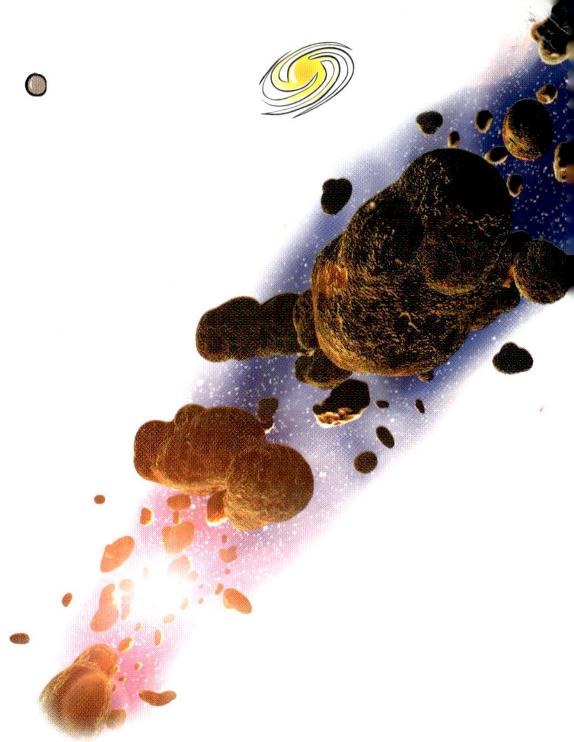

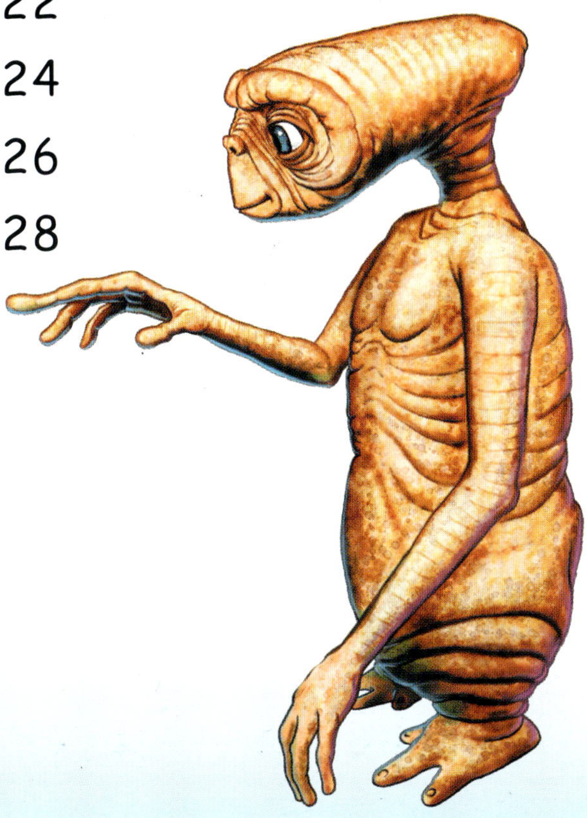

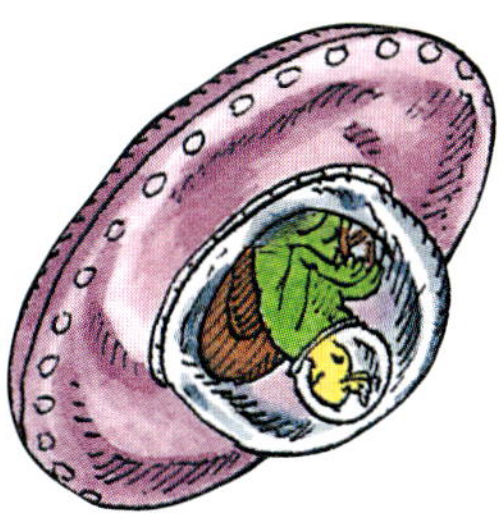

The Solar System

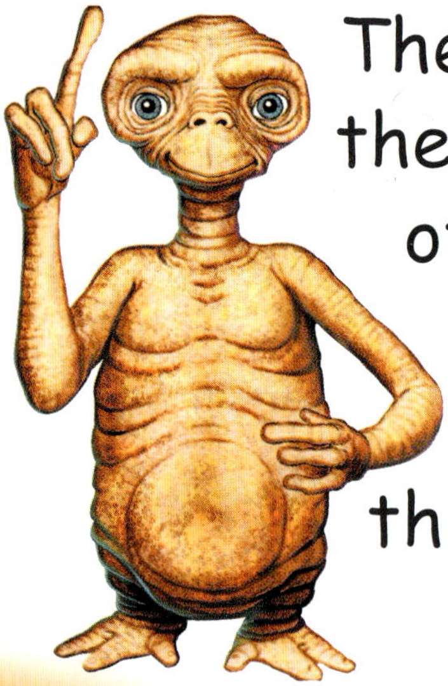

The Solar System is the Sun, the Earth, the other planets, their moons and all the other objects that move through space with the Sun. E.T. loves to watch it through his telescope!

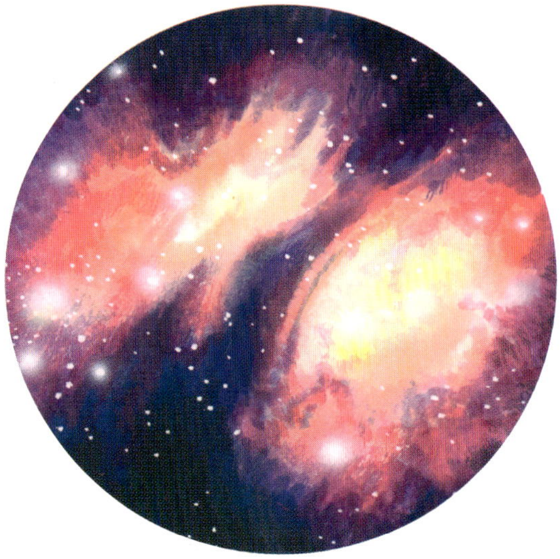

The start of the Solar System

About five billion years ago, clumps of matter started to come together inside a vast, spinning disc of gas, dust and ice. The clumps grew as more gas, dust and ice stuck to them. Millions of years later, the biggest clump, in the middle, became the Sun. Others became the nine planets of the Solar System.

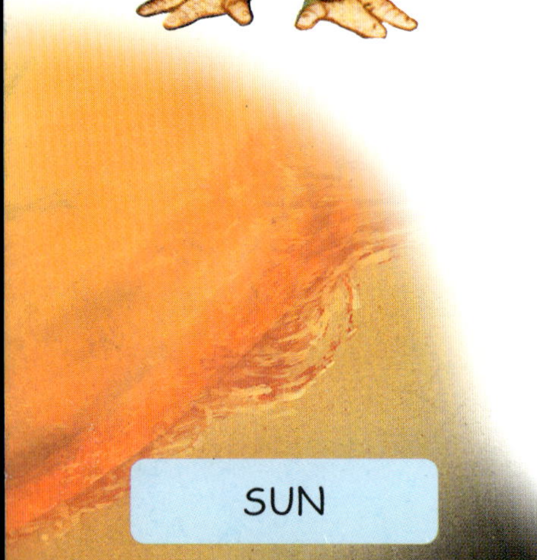

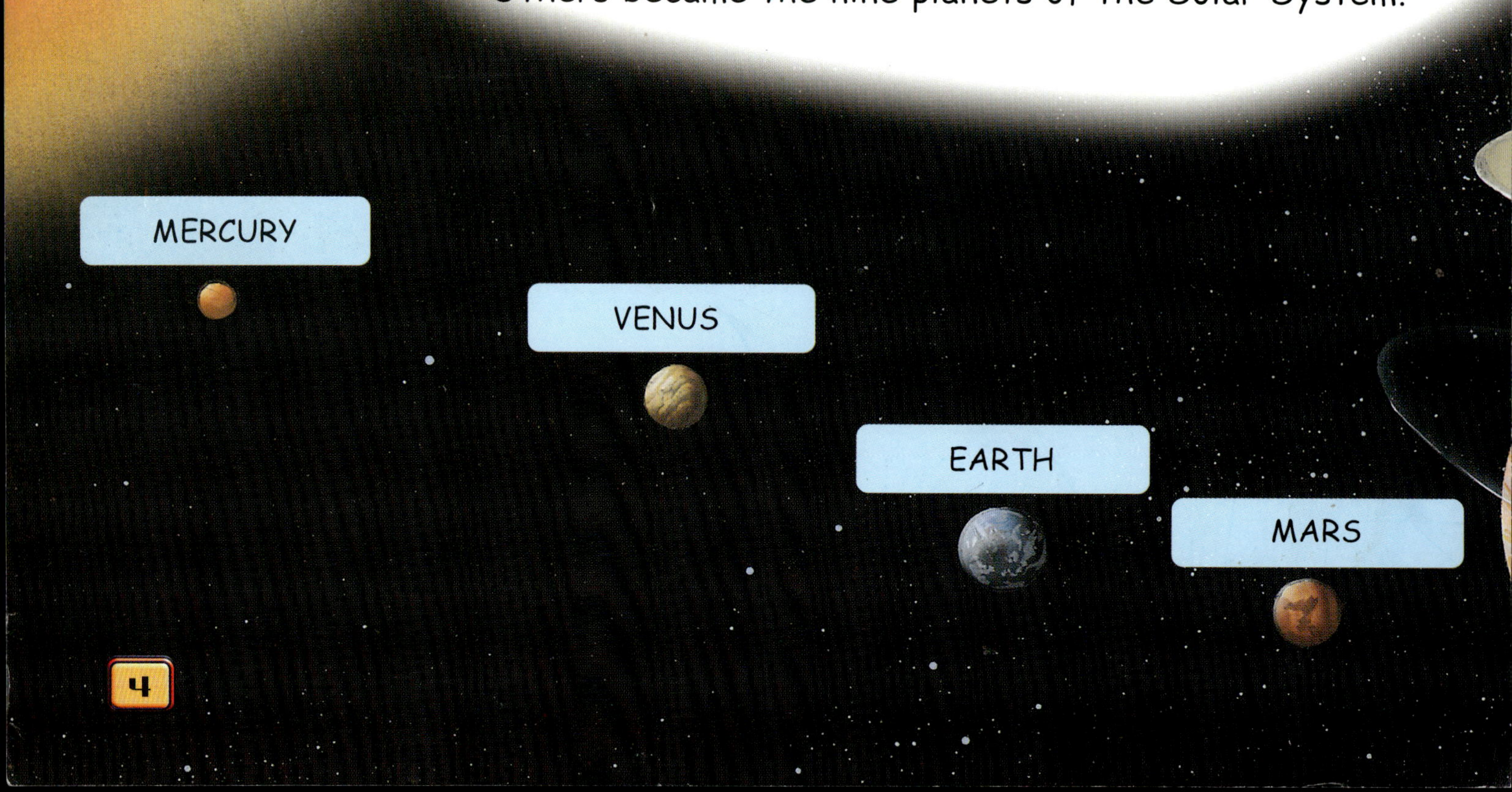

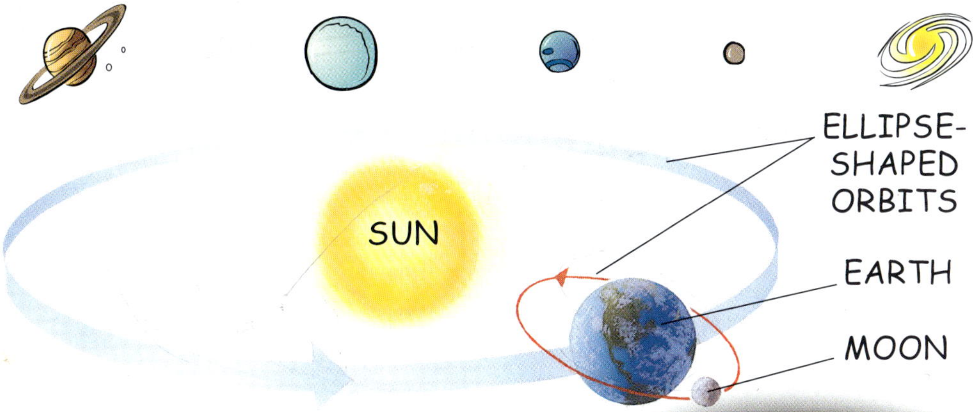

The planets travel around the Sun, and the moons travel around the planets. Their paths are called orbits. Orbits are the shape of squashed circles, called ellipses.

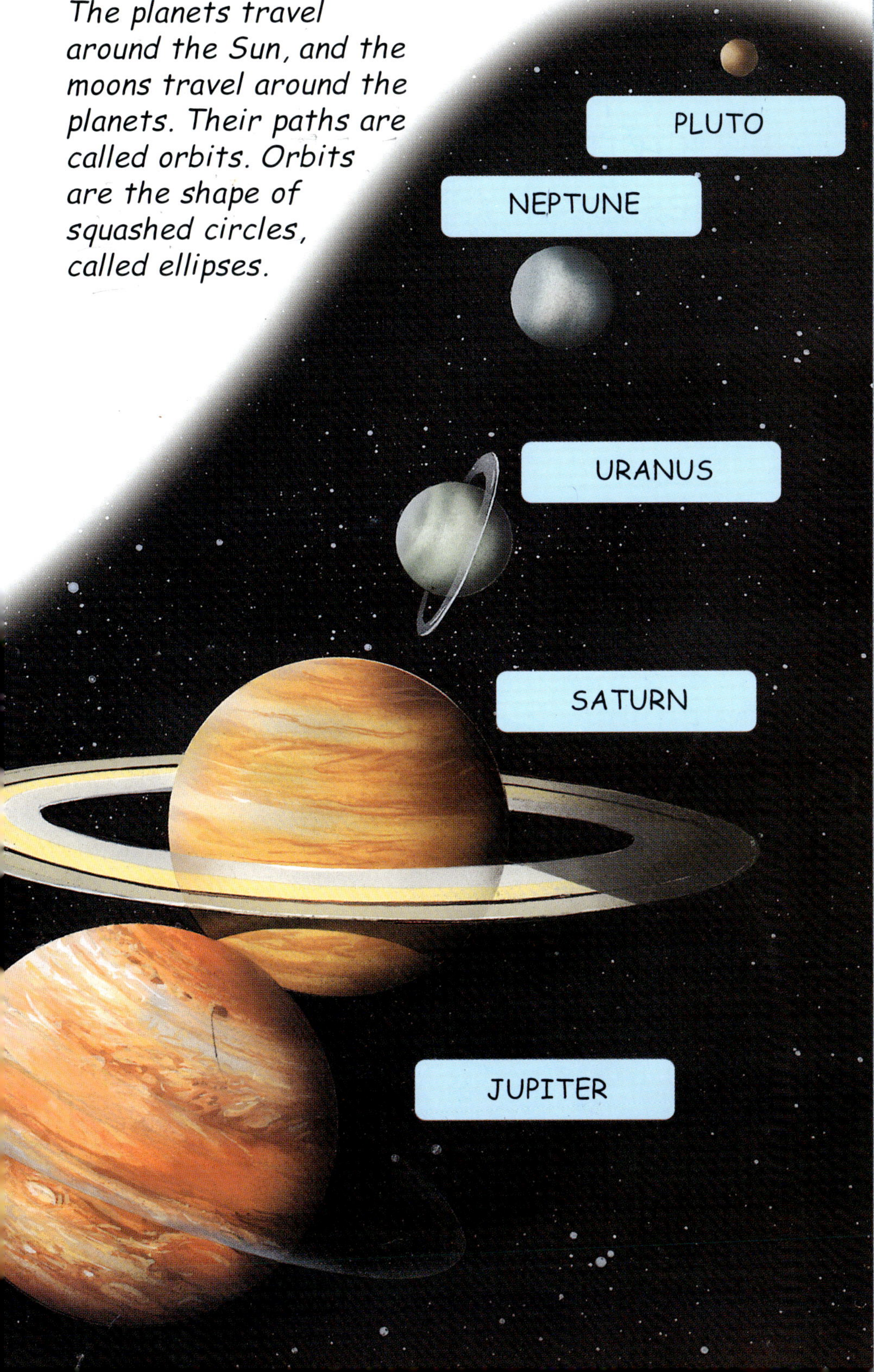

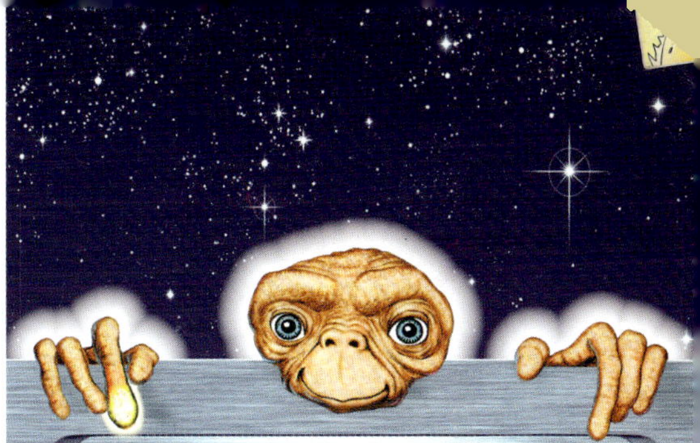

INFORMATION OVERLOAD!

E.T. has collected so many fascinating facts that he must send them back to his planet to be analysed.

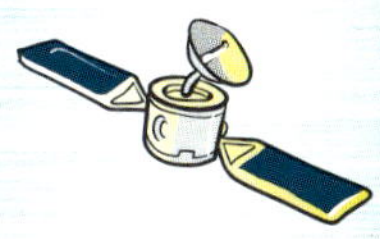

After the planets formed, rocks still kept crashing into them from space. The rocks made shallow marks called craters in the surfaces of the planets.

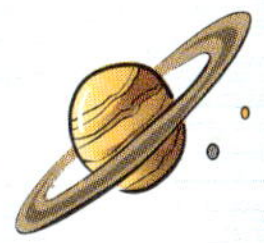

Thousands of small pieces of rock and ice left over from the start of the Solar System still circle the Sun.

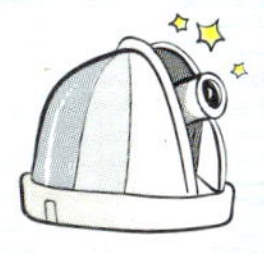

Astronomers have discovered more than 60 moons orbiting the nine planets. They expect to discover more.

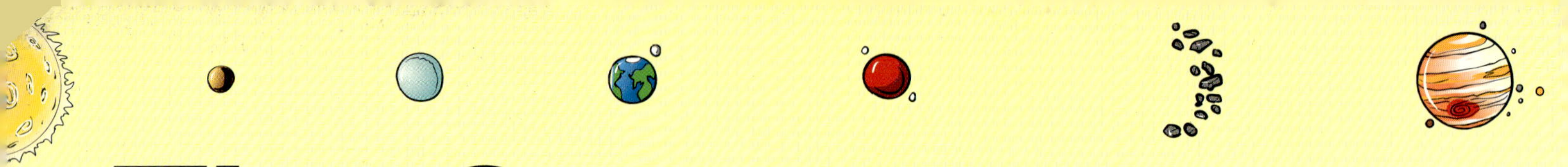

The Sun

The Sun is the nearest star to the Earth. It is made mostly from a gas called hydrogen. The Sun burns all the time, and shines because it is so hot. The temperature at its centre is about 15 million°C! E.T. knows that this is more than 60,000 times hotter than even the hottest kitchen oven.

WARNING!
NEVER look directly at the Sun. It is so bright that it can damage your eyes very seriously.

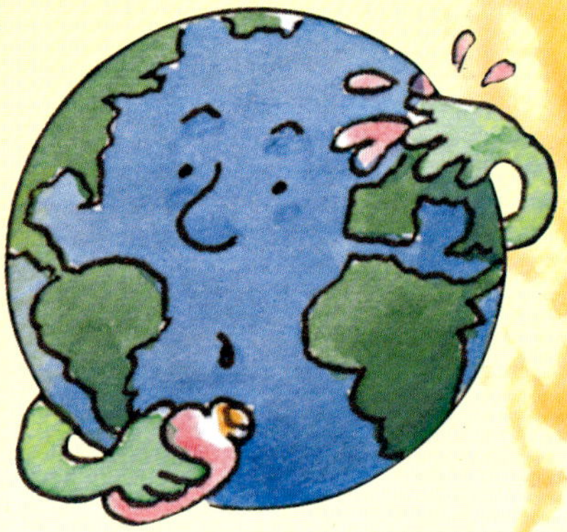

The air around the Earth traps some of the Sun's heat and stops it escaping back into space. This helps keep the Earth warm.

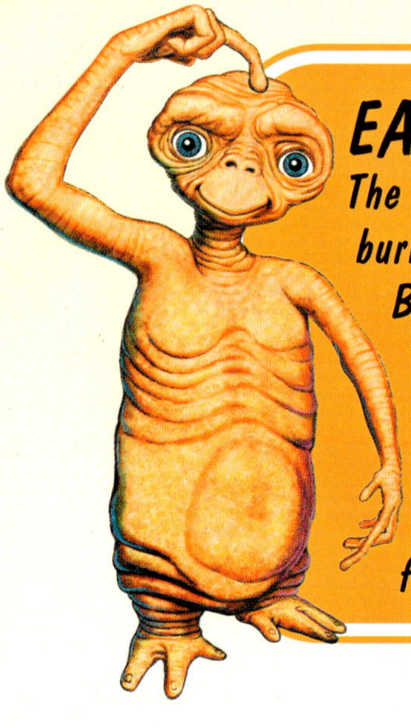

EARTH ALERT!
The Sun is gradually burning itself away. But there is no need to worry just yet. It will carry on shining for about another five billion years.

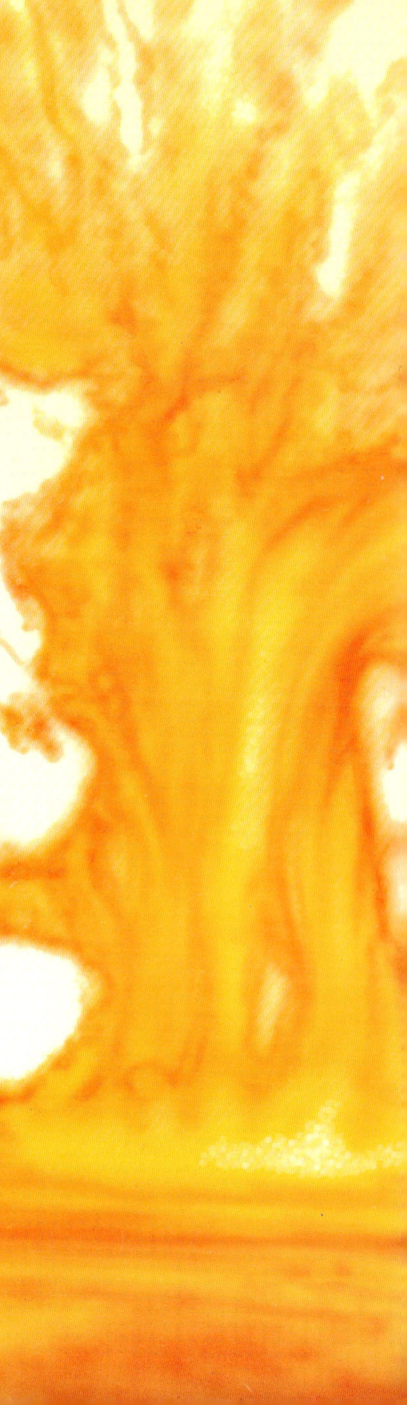

Fiery flares full of energy sometimes erupt from the Sun's surface.

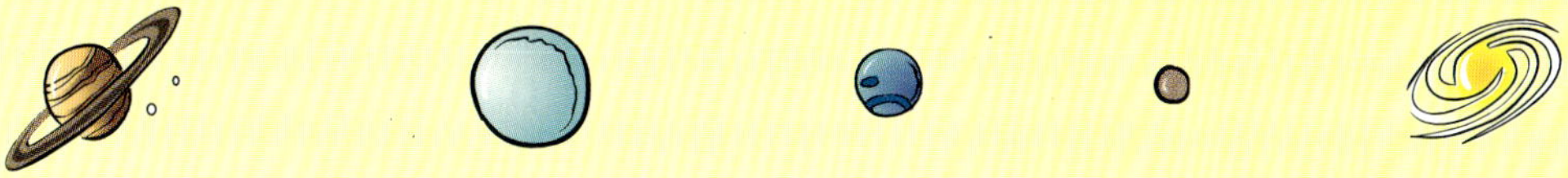

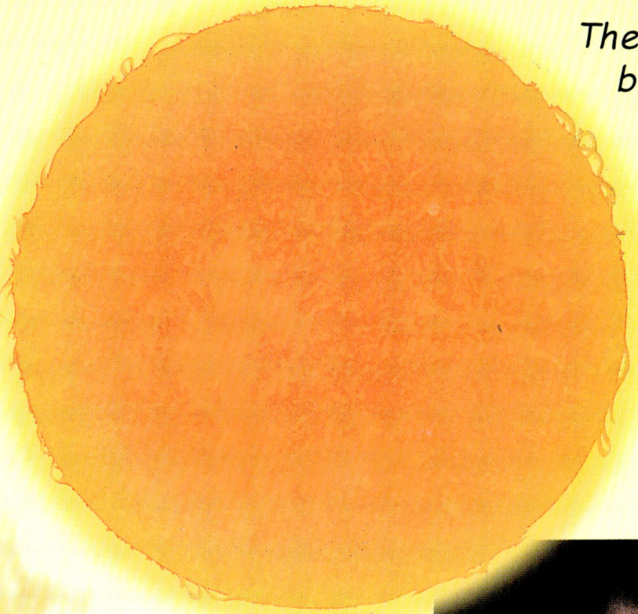

The Sun is a giant boiling ball of gas. It is so big that it contains as much matter as 333,000 Earths.

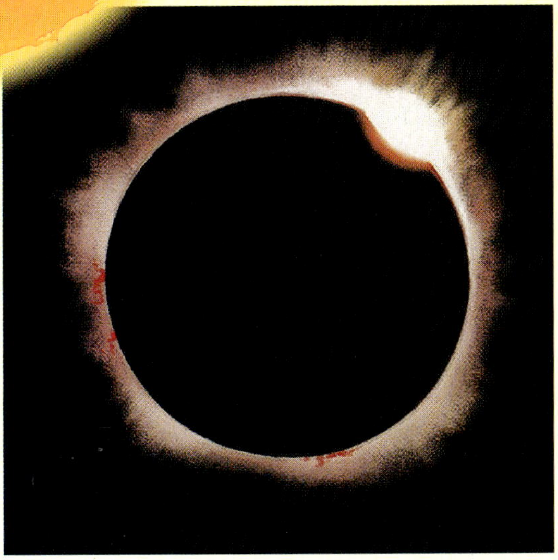

Solar eclipses

About once each year, the Earth's Moon comes between the Earth and the Sun, and blots out the Sun's light. This is called a solar eclipse.

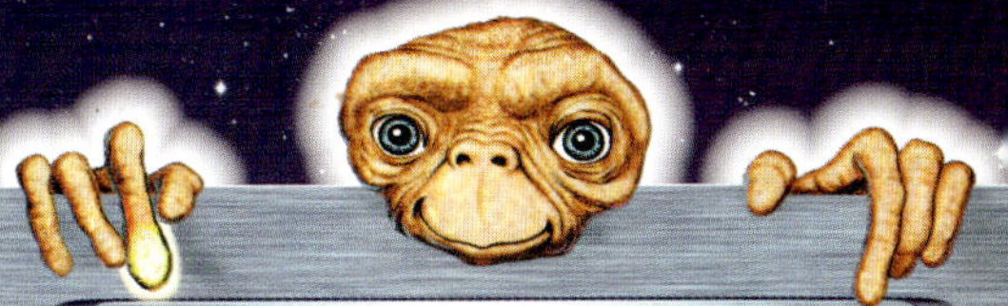

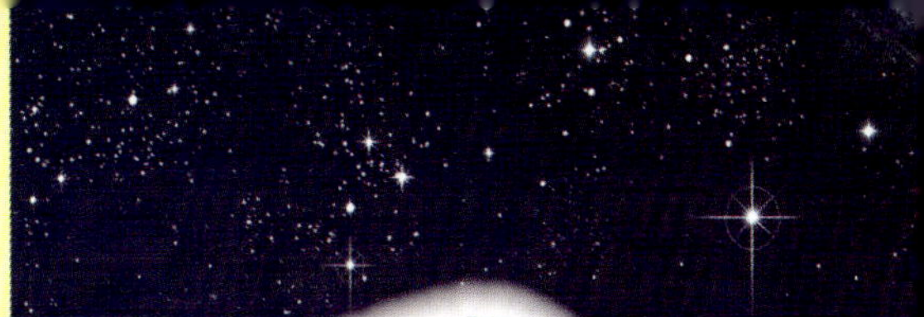

INFORMATION OVERLOAD!

E.T. has collected so many fascinating facts that he must send them back to his planet to be analysed.

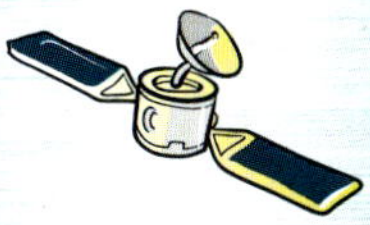

The Sun is about 150 million kilometres away from the Earth.

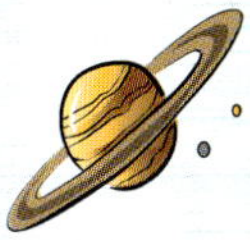

Sunlight travels 300,000 kilometres every second. It takes 8 minutes and 20 seconds to reach the Earth.

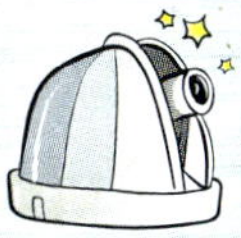

Sunspots are dark patches on the Sun's surface. They are cooler than the other areas around them. Each spot lasts for a few weeks, then disappears.

The Earth

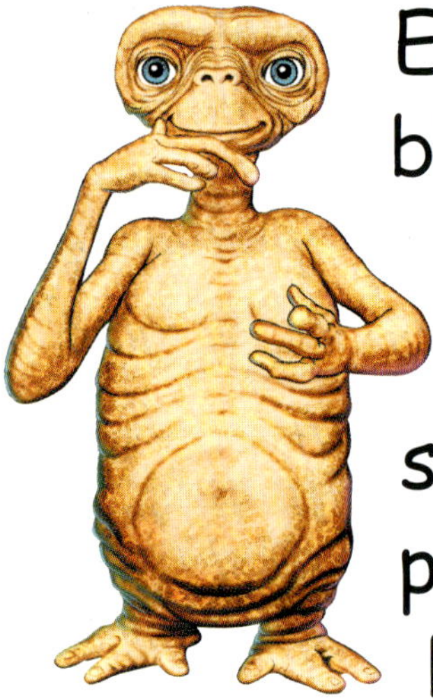

E.T. thinks the Earth looks like a blue jewel hanging in the blackness of space. It is the only planet with running water on its surface, an atmosphere with plenty of oxygen gas for breathing, and the right amount of heat and light for life.

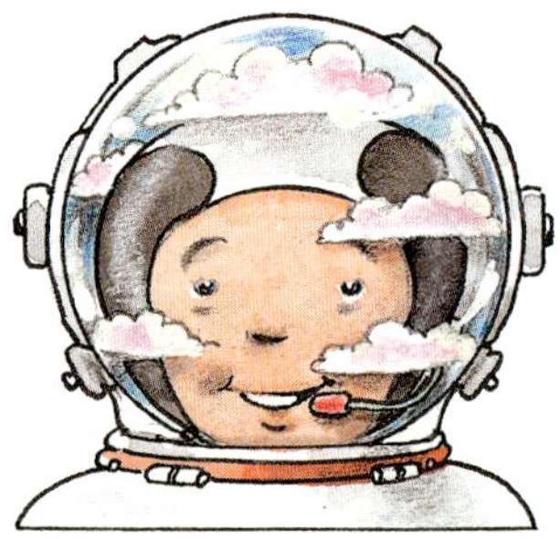

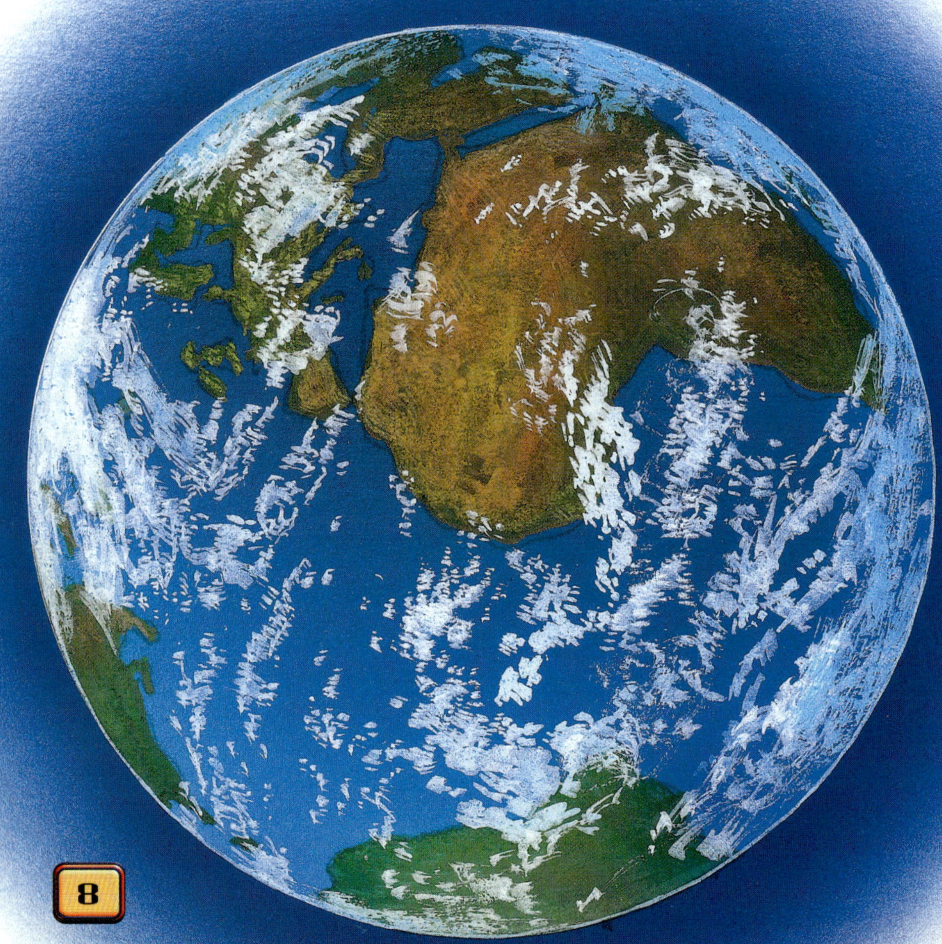

The atmosphere

An atmosphere is the layer of gases that surrounds a planet. The Earth has a thick atmosphere. As well as the gases nitrogen and oxygen, it contains water vapour. This rises from the oceans when the Sun warms them.

The blue oceans make the Earth one of the most colourful planets.

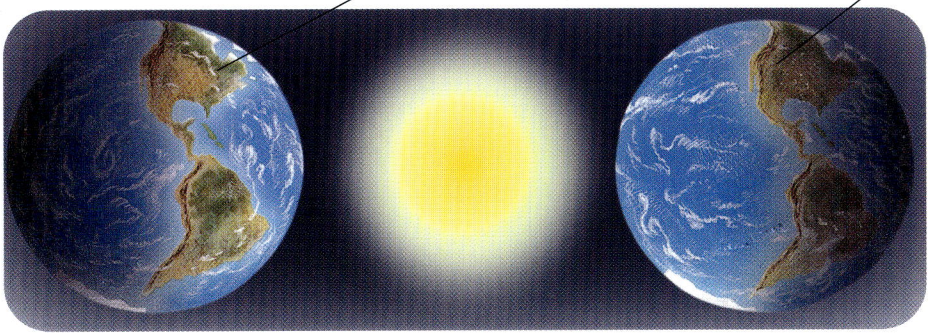

Night and day

The Earth spins round once every day, always moving towards the east. As it spins, places facing the Sun slowly turn away from it so that day becomes night. At the same time, places that were in the dark slowly turn towards the Sun, and night becomes day.

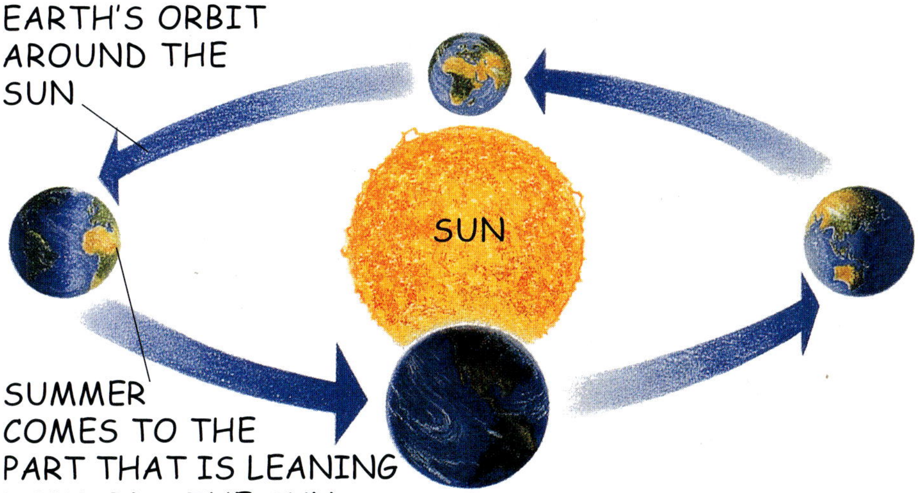

The seasons

The Earth orbits the Sun once a year. For six months, the top half of the planet leans towards the Sun, making it spring, then summer there. For the other six months, it leans away, making it autumn, then winter. The opposite happens in the Earth's bottom half, so it has opposite seasons.

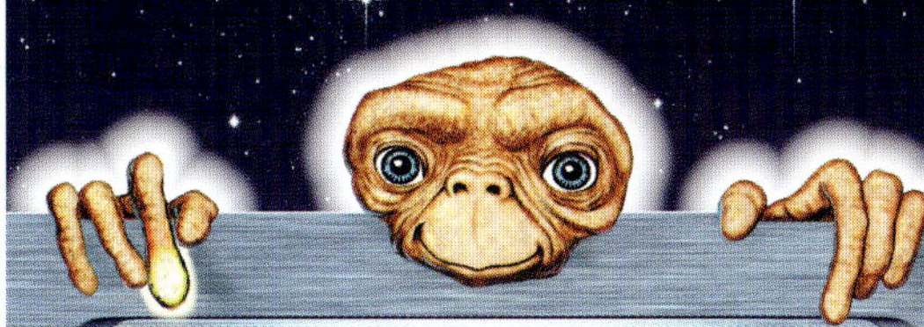

INFORMATION OVERLOAD!

E.T. has collected so many fascinating facts that he must send them back to his planet to be analysed.

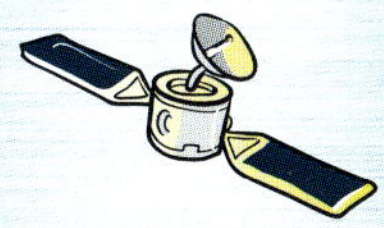

Oceans, seas and other waters cover nearly three-quarters of the Earth's surface.

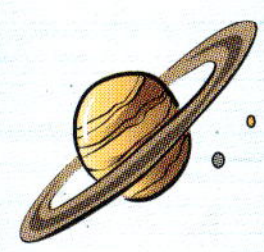

The Earth's centre is solid metal, mostly iron. It has liquid metal all round it.

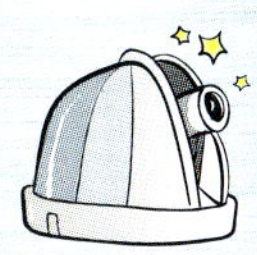

The sunniest place on the Earth is Yuma, in Arizona, USA. It has more than 4,000 hours of sunshine every year.

Moon Missions

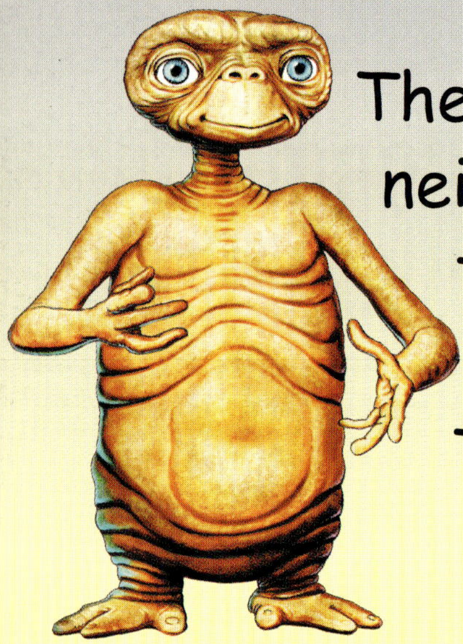

The Moon is the Earth's closest neighbour. E.T. likes to go there to leave footprints. The USA landed the first astronauts on the Moon on July 20, 1969.

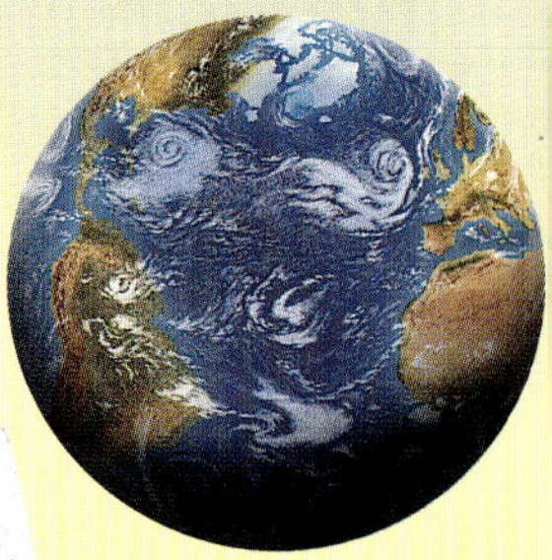

Astronauts collect rocks and take photographs on the Moon.

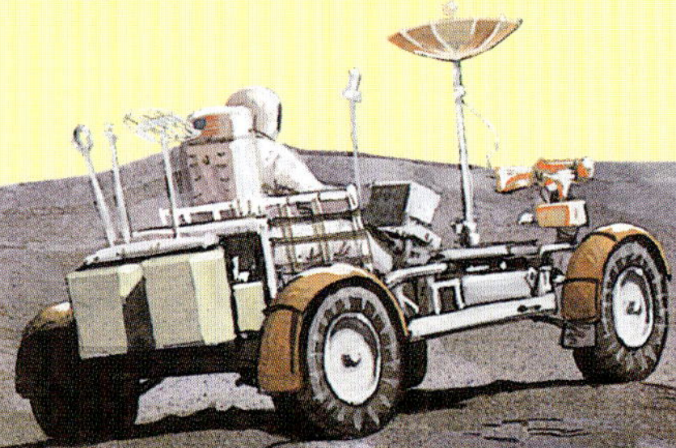

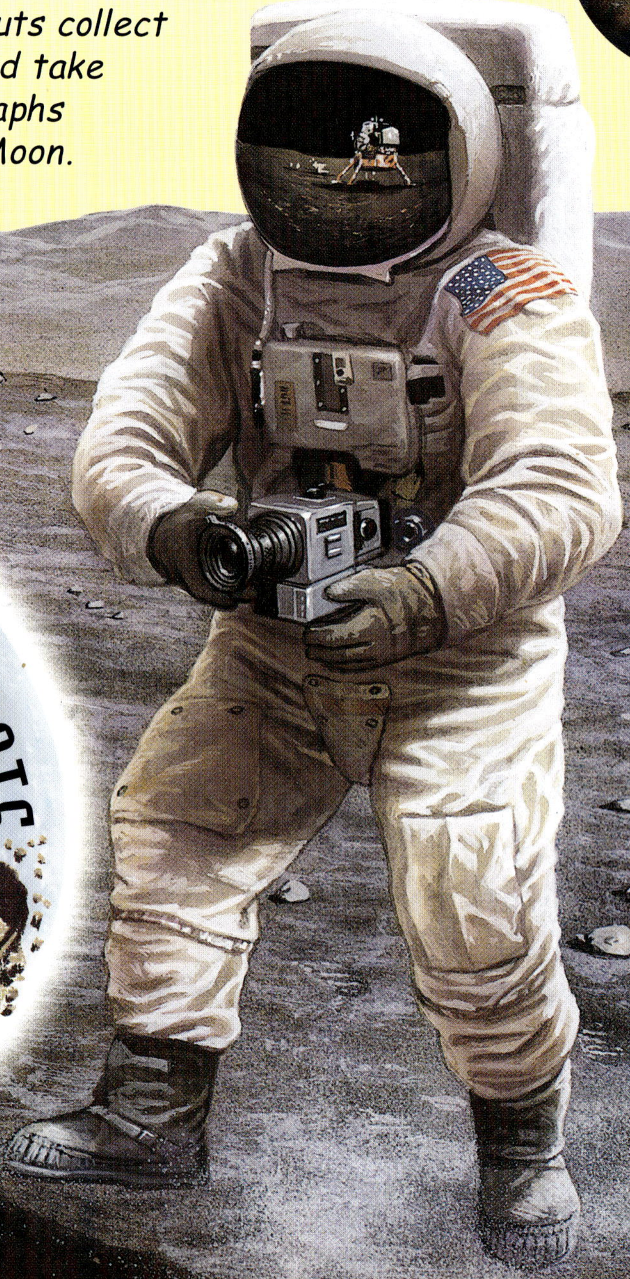

PHONE HOME FACTS

There is no atmosphere on the Moon and no weather. Without any wind or rain to disturb them, the astronauts' footprints will stay in place for about 100 years.

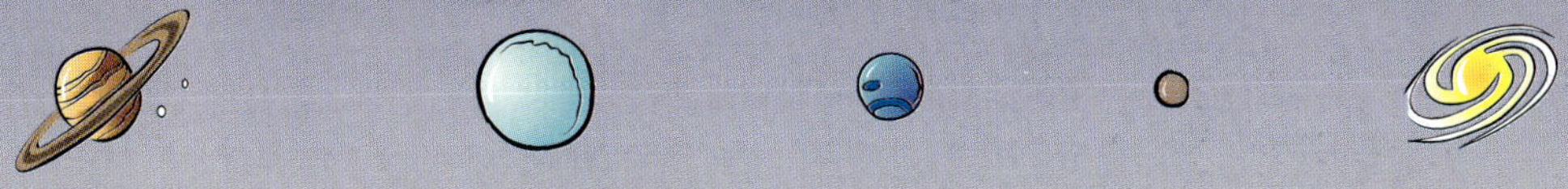

Rocky surface

The surface of the Moon is not flat and smooth, but rocky with lots of craters. From Earth, they look like hundreds of small, dark patches all over the Moon's disc.

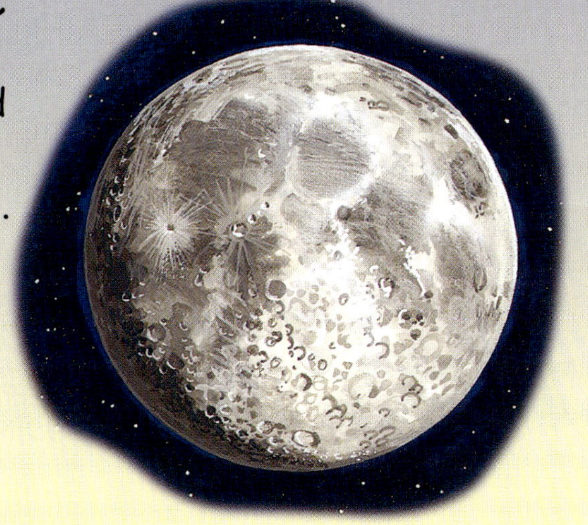

Changing shape

The Moon orbits the Earth about once a month. As it does so, it seems to change shape. This is because people on the Earth can see only the part of the Moon that is lit by the Sun. The sunlit part changes as the Moon circles our planet.

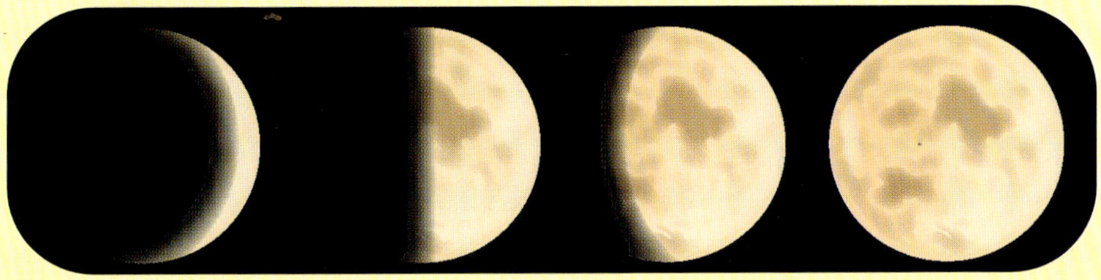

Pulling power

Everything in space has a pulling force called gravity. Gravity holds things together and stops them floating away into space. When a planet and a moon are close enough, there is a pulling contest between their forces of gravity, like a tug-of-war.

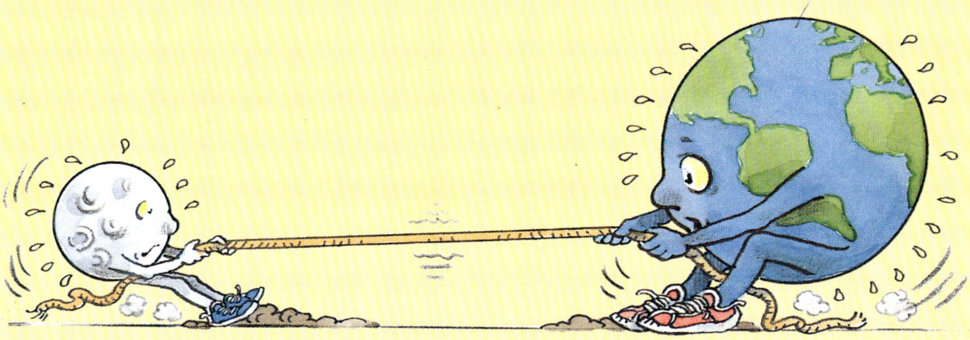

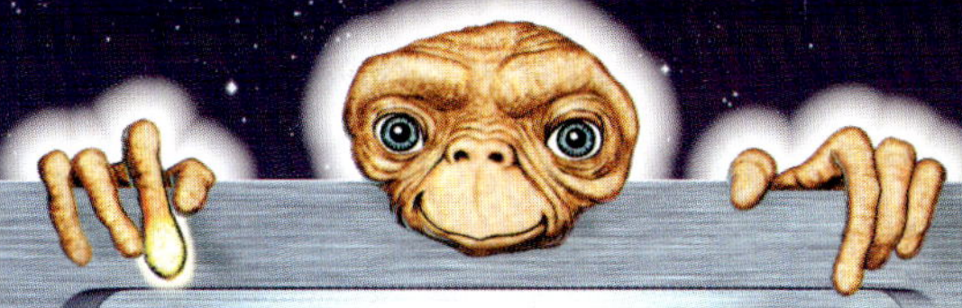

INFORMATION OVERLOAD!

E.T. has collected so many fascinating facts that he must send them back to his planet to be analysed.

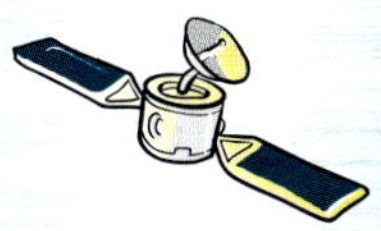

In total, 12 US astronauts have landed on the Moon, from six different space missions.

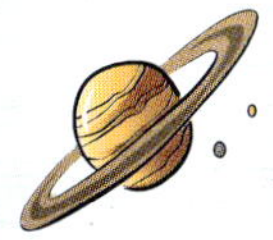

US astronaut Neil Armstrong was the very first person to walk on the Moon.

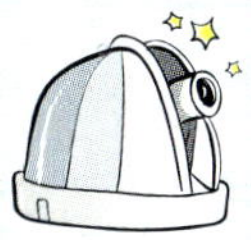

From the Earth, we can always see only one side of the Moon. The other, far side was photographed by the Soviet space probe *Luna 3* in 1959.

Rocky Worlds

Five of the nine planets are made of rock. One is the Earth, our home planet. The others are Mercury, Venus, Mars and Pluto. E.T. has discovered that these four small, rocky worlds are all very different from each other.

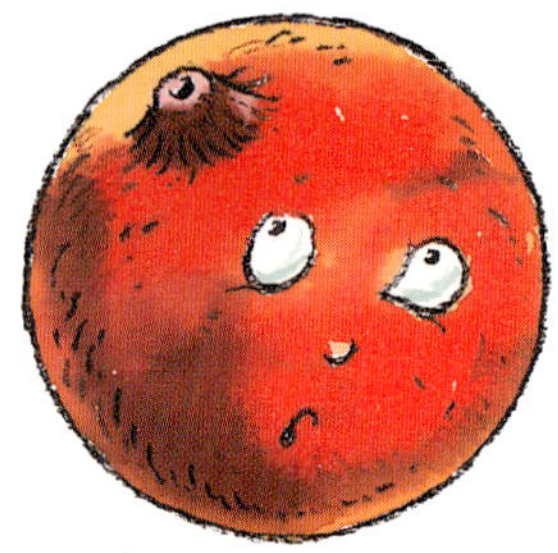

The biggest volcano in the Solar System is Olympus Mons on Mars. It is 26,400 metres high. This is more than three times higher than Everest, the Earth's tallest mountain.

Hot and cold

Mercury is so close to the Sun that the planet's atmosphere boiled away into space many millions of years ago. The side of Mercury that is turned towards the Sun is heated to more than 450°C. The other side is freezing cold.

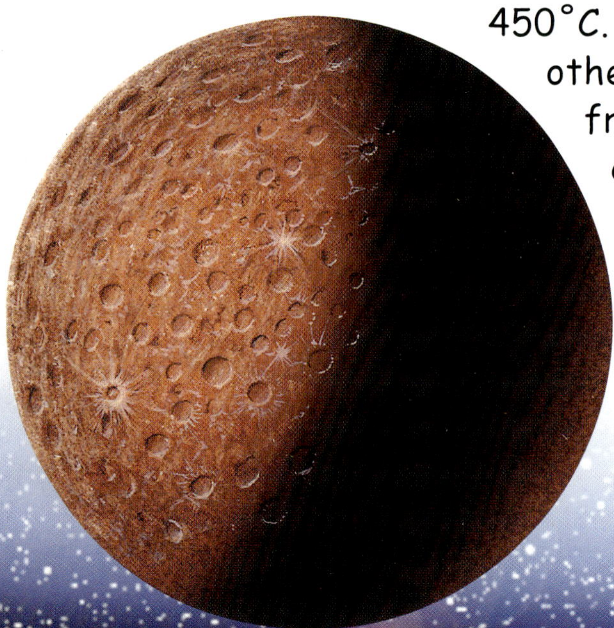

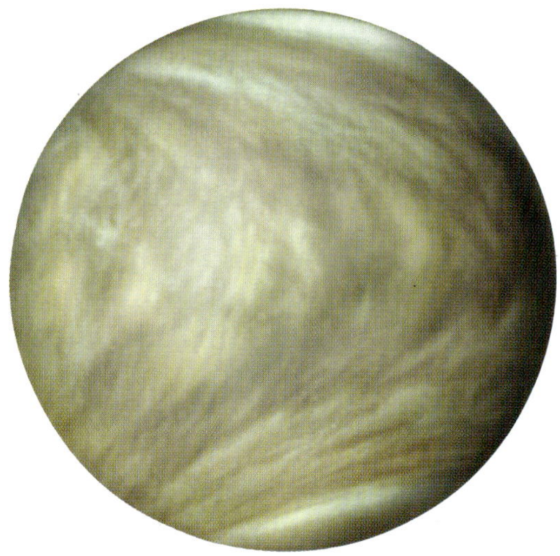

Hot spot

Venus is the hottest planet because it has a thick atmosphere that traps the Sun's heat. Its surface reaches 480°C.

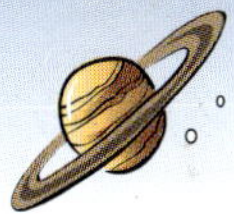

Red rocks

Mars is the most Earthlike planet. It is called the Red Planet because its surface is covered with red rocks and dust.

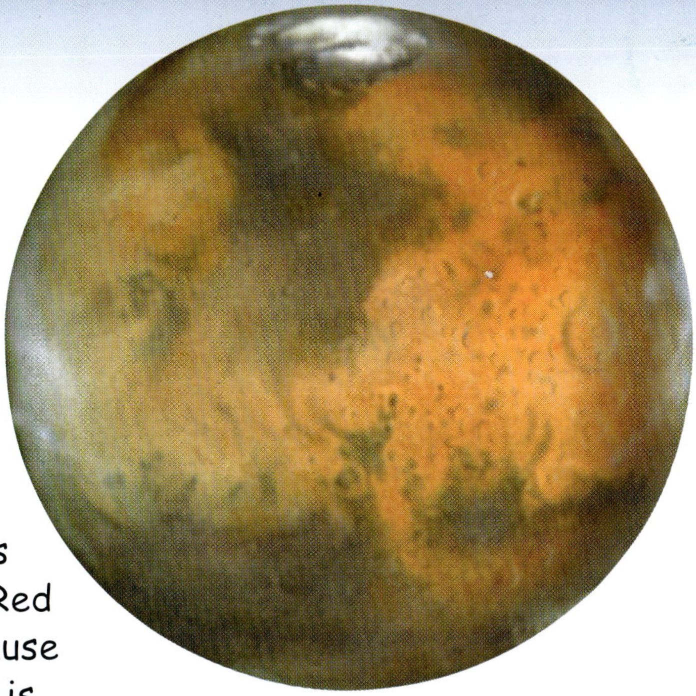

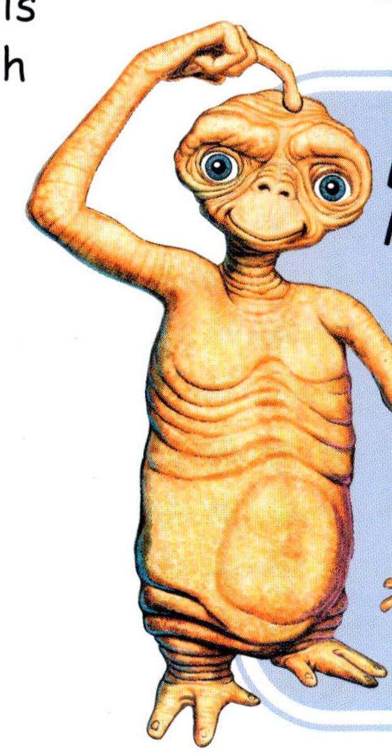

EARTH ALERT!

None of the rocky worlds are suitable for humans to live on. Some are too hot, some are too cold, some have a poisonous atmosphere – and others have no atmosphere at all!

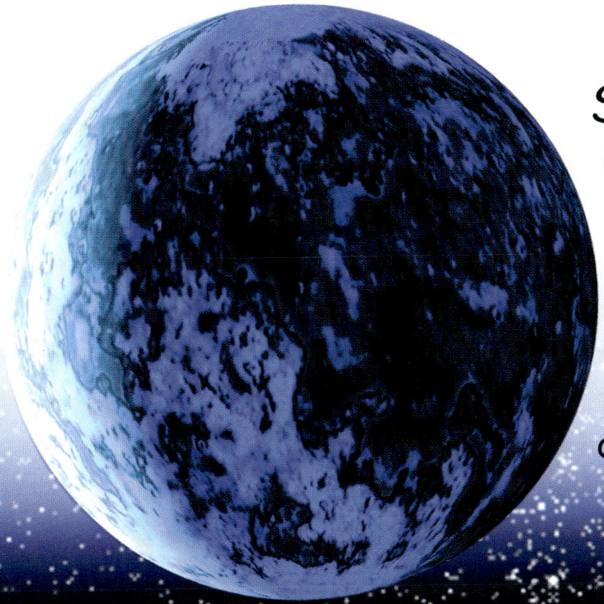

Slow turn

Pluto is so far away from the Sun that it takes 248 years to go round it just once. The Earth takes one year.

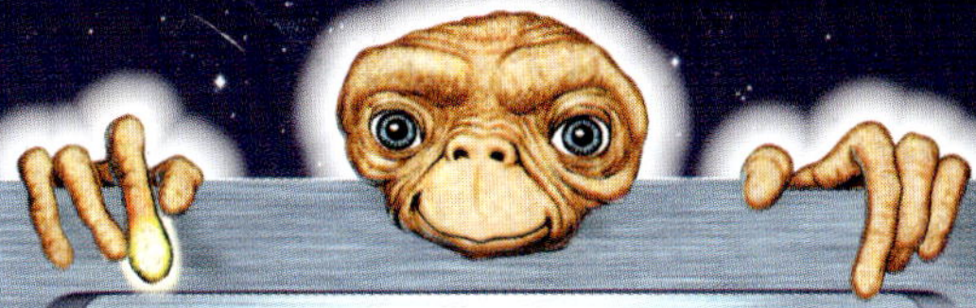

INFORMATION OVERLOAD!

E.T. has collected so many fascinating facts that he must send them back to his planet to be analysed.

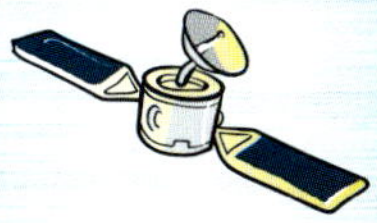

Mercury races round the Sun in only 88 days. If it went any slower, it would fall into the Sun and disappear.

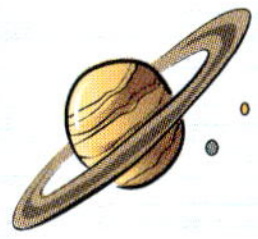

Winds on Mars often blow up dust storms that cover the whole planet.

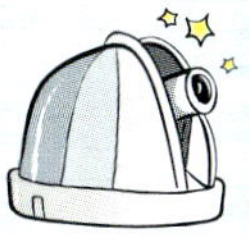

If you could stand on the surface of Venus, you would be squashed by the atmosphere, boiled in the heat and burned by acid rain falling from the clouds.

Gas Giants

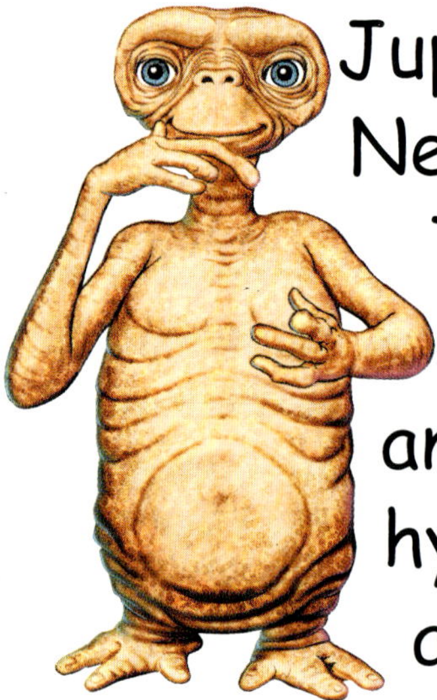

Jupiter, Saturn, Uranus and Neptune are called gas giants. This is because they are by far the biggest planets, and are made mostly of hydrogen gas. Hydrogen is also the gas that makes up the Sun. E.T. has learned that the gas giants all have rings of rock and ice around them.

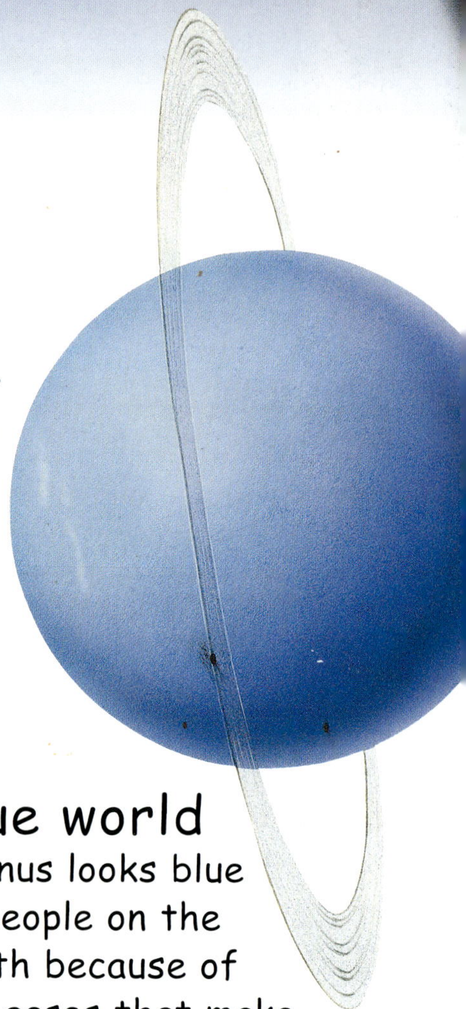

Blue world

Uranus looks blue to people on the Earth because of the gases that make it up. The planet is also tipped over so that it orbits the Sun on its side instead of upright.

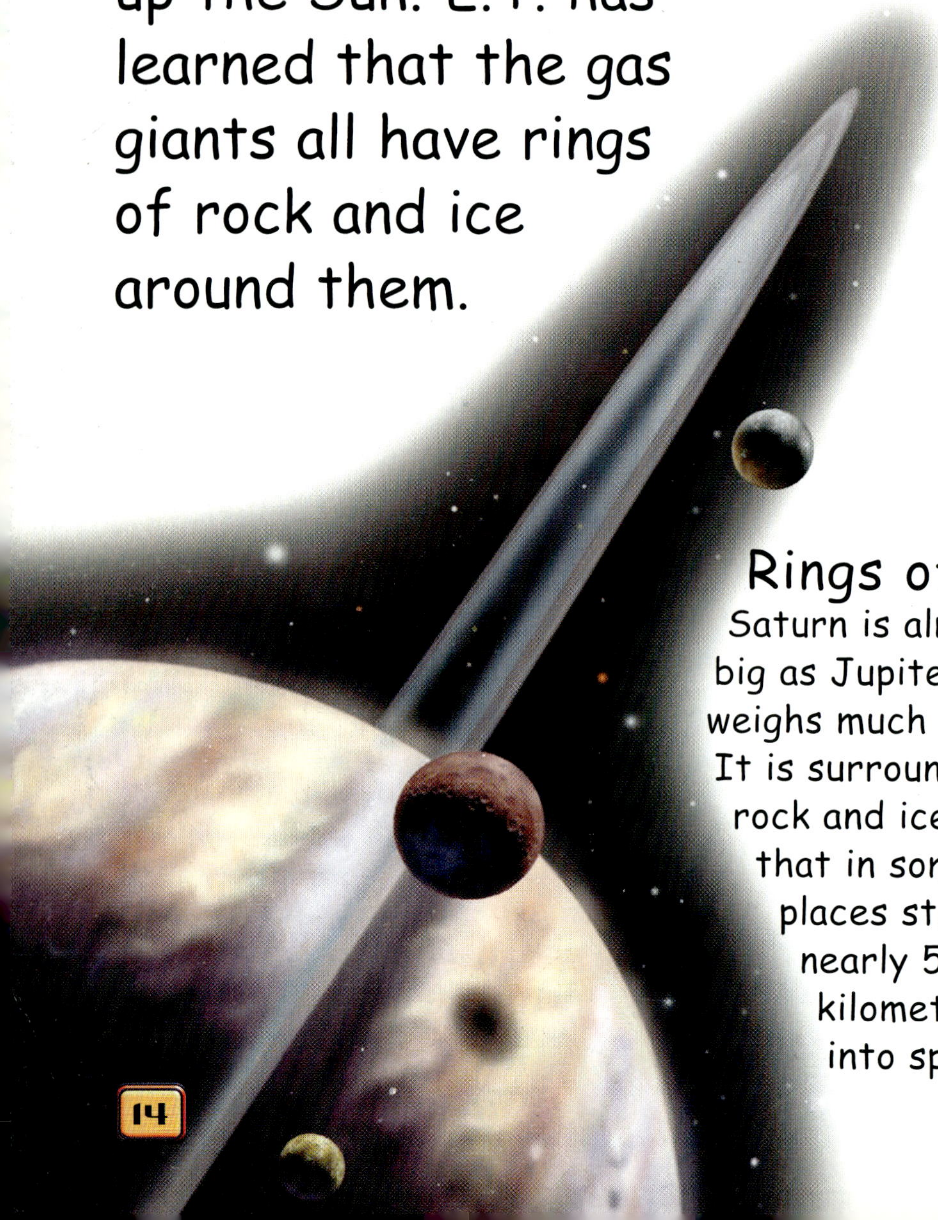

Rings of ice

Saturn is almost as big as Jupiter, but weighs much less. It is surrounded by rock and ice rings that in some places stretch nearly 500,000 kilometres out into space.

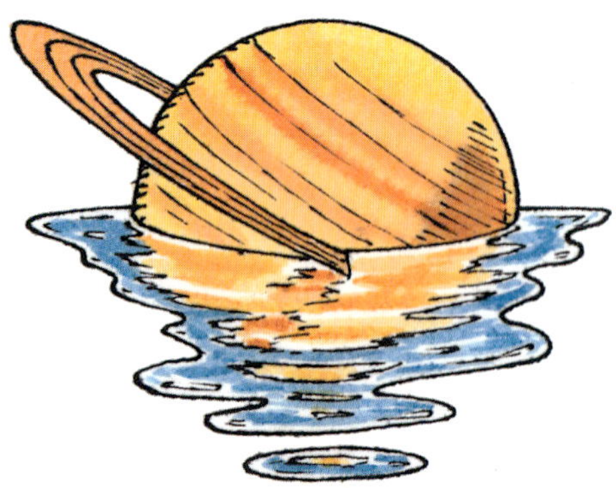

If you could find a sea big enough to put it in, Saturn is so light that it would float.

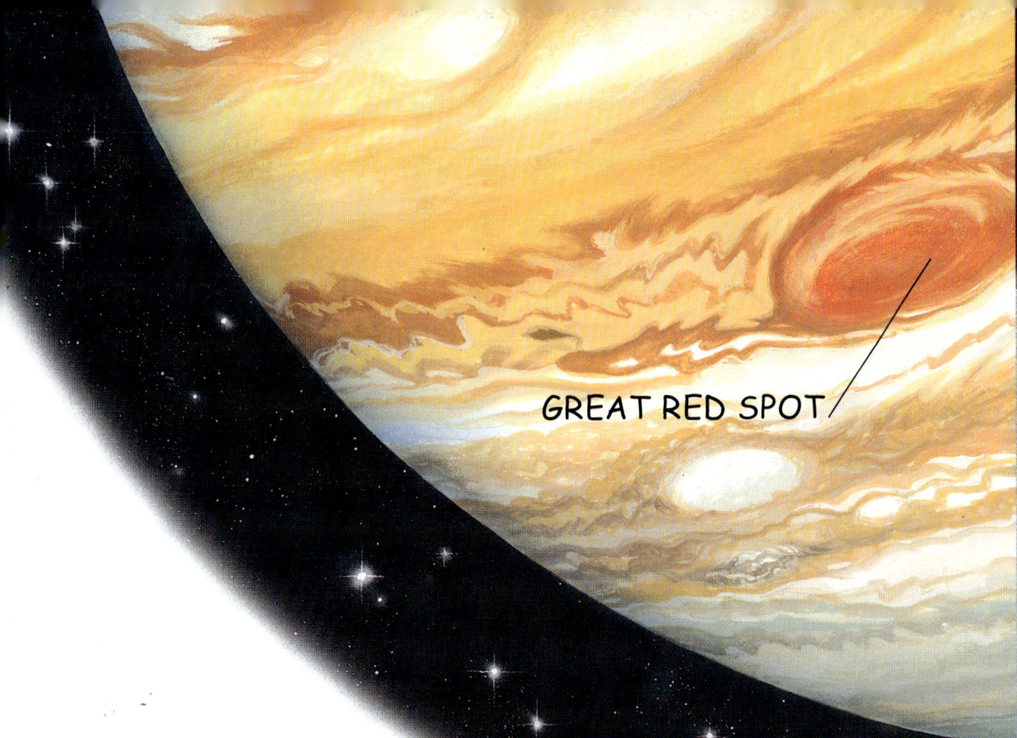

Giant Jupiter

Jupiter is the biggest planet. More than 1,300 Earths would fit inside it. A huge storm, the Great Red Spot, has raged on Jupiter for more than 300 years.

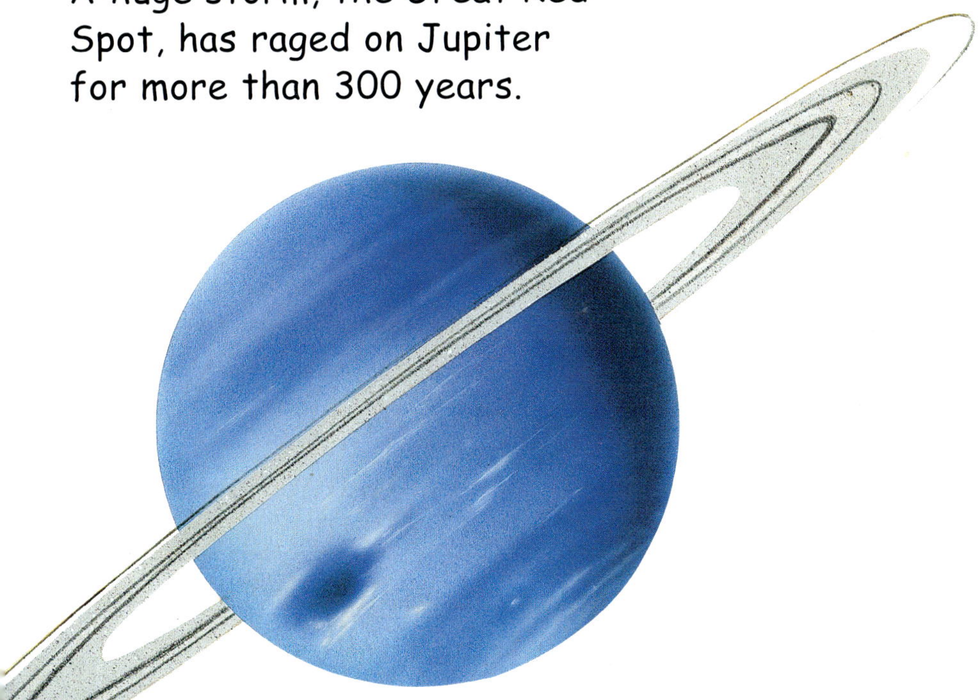

Stormy planet

Neptune is a blue planet like Uranus, but has stormier weather. It receives 1,000 times less heat from the Sun than the Earth does.

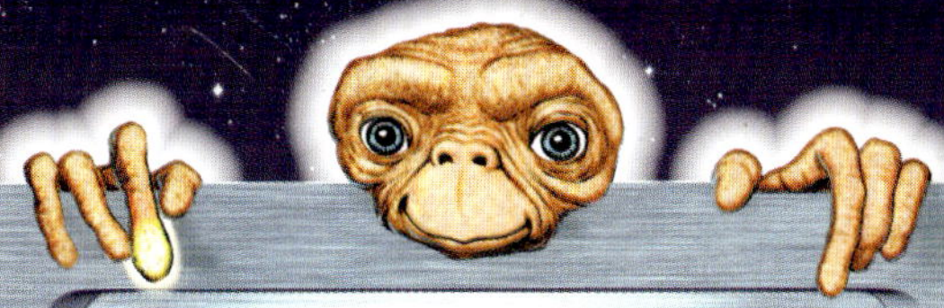

INFORMATION OVERLOAD!

E.T. has collected so many fascinating facts that he must send them back to his planet to be analysed.

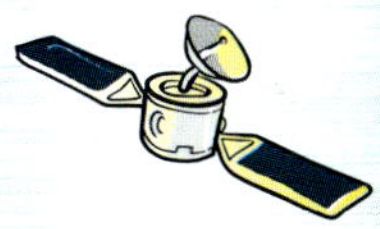

The fastest winds in the Solar System blow around Saturn. They are ten times faster than the strongest winds on the Earth.

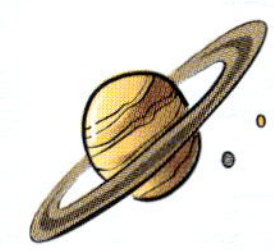

Jupiter's moon Ganymede is the biggest moon in the Solar System. It is even bigger than the planet Mercury.

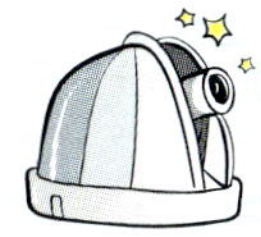

Neptune's biggest moon, Triton, flies around Neptune backwards! The planet's seven other moons travel in the opposite direction.

Comets

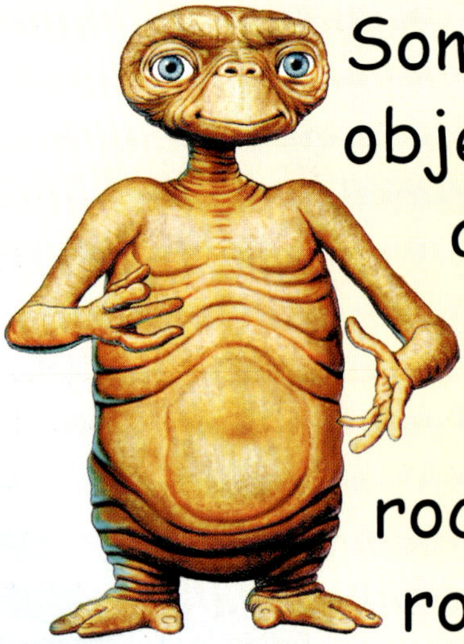

Sometimes a bright object called a comet appears in the sky – E.T. has seen one! Comets are balls of rock and ice that fly round the Sun. As they near the Sun, they warm up and give off gas and dust. The gas and dust form two tails.

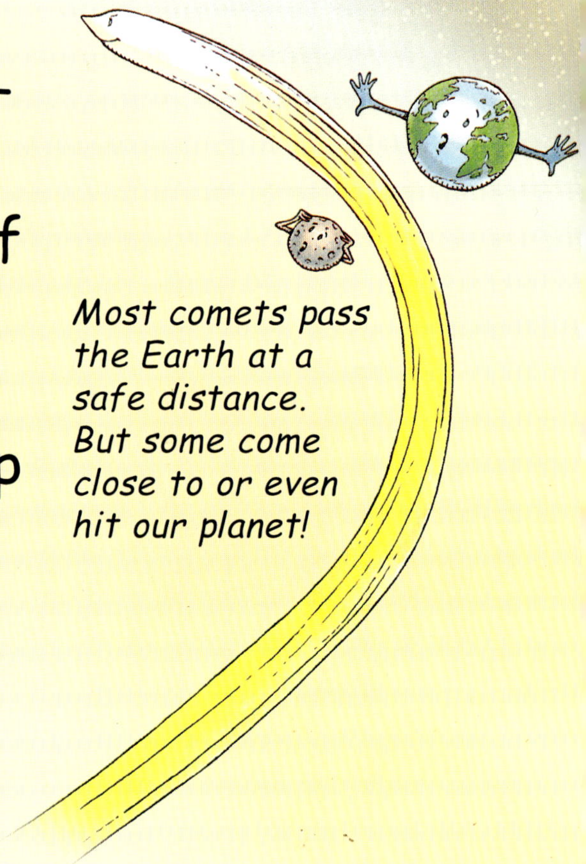

Most comets pass the Earth at a safe distance. But some come close to or even hit our planet!

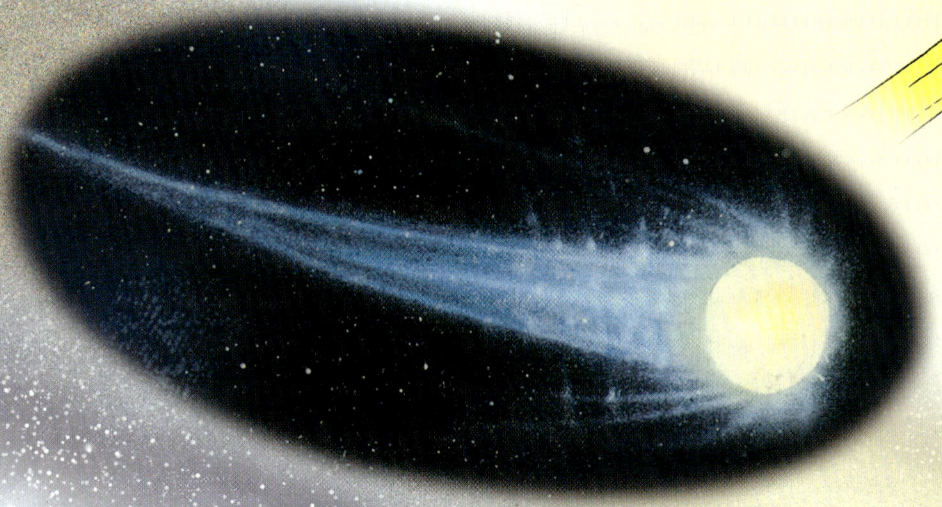

Comet tails always point away from the Sun because particles from the Sun sweep them backwards.

Halley's Comet

More than 300 years ago, an astronomer called Edmond Halley saw a comet in the sky. He was the first person to realize that it came back every 76 years. This comet is now named after him. It last appeared in 1986.

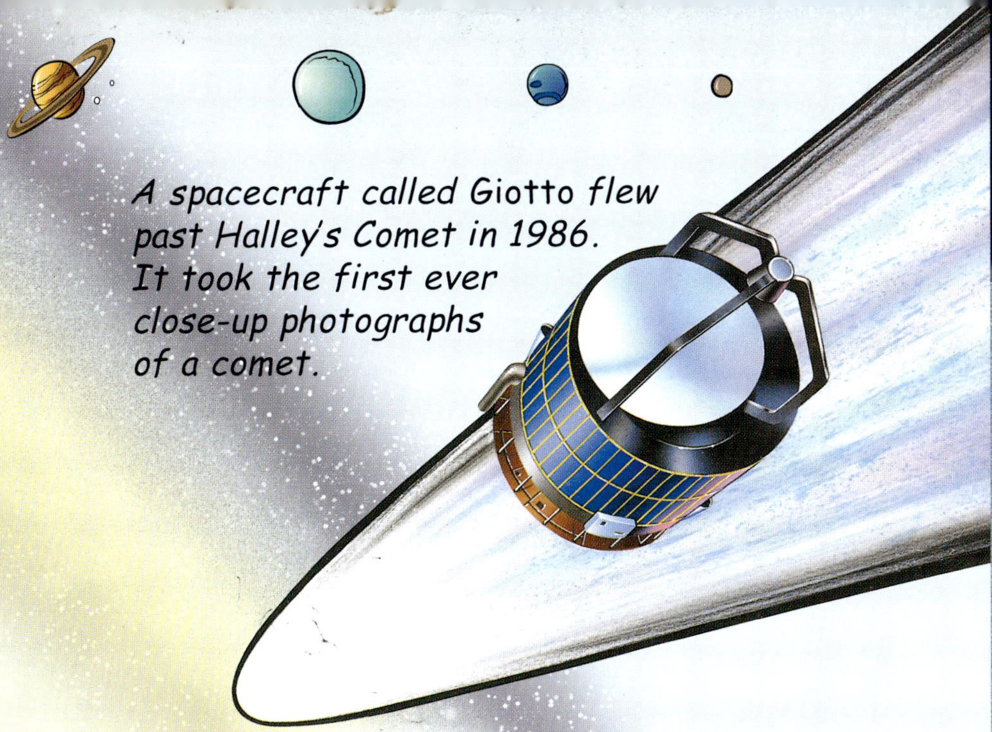

A spacecraft called Giotto flew past Halley's Comet in 1986. It took the first ever close-up photographs of a comet.

PHONE HOME FACTS

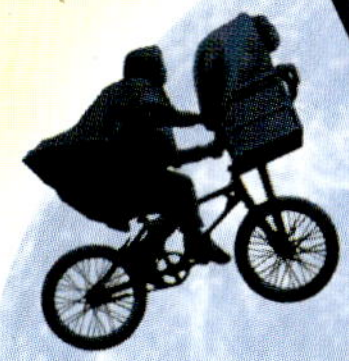

American Gene Shoemaker was one of the men who discovered Comet Shoemaker-Levy 9. After he died in 1997, a space probe carried his ashes to the Moon.

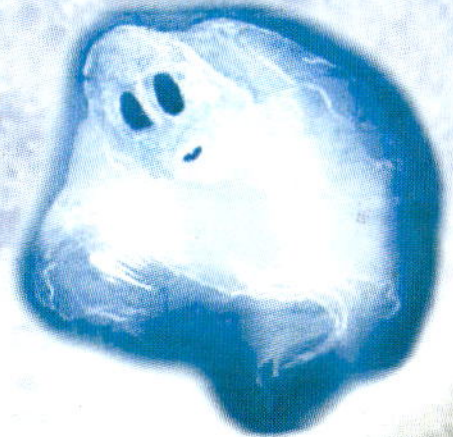

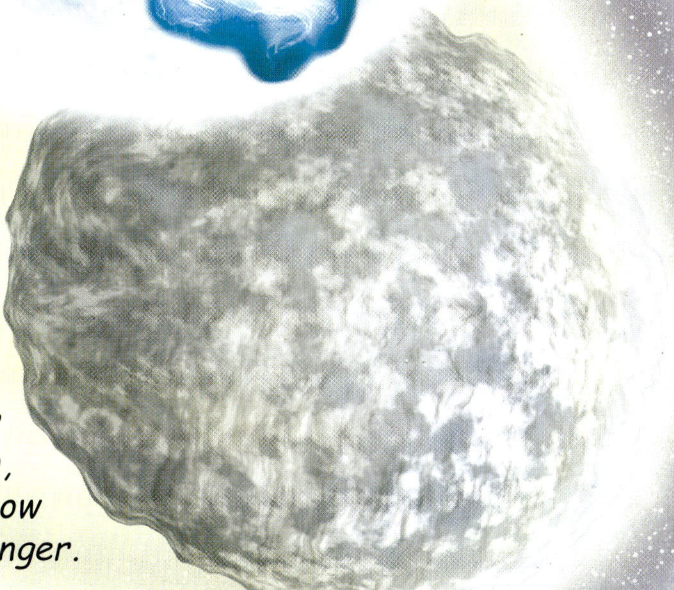

As a comet gets closer to the Sun, its tails grow steadily longer.

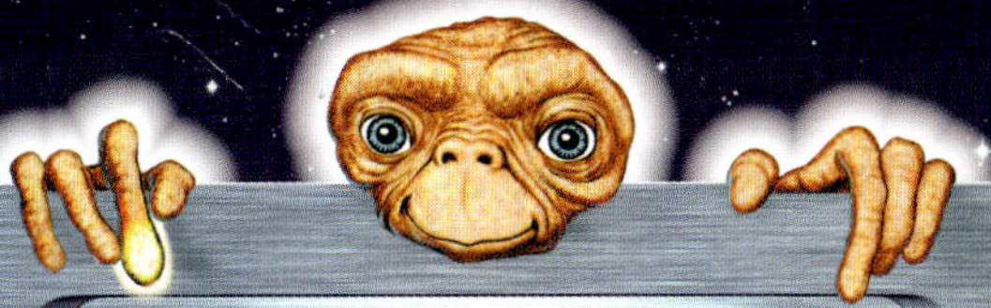

INFORMATION OVERLOAD!

E.T. has collected so many fascinating facts that he must send them back to his planet to be analysed.

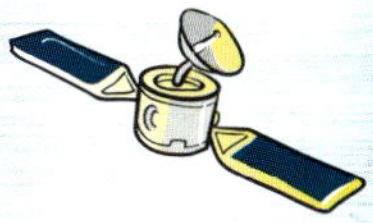

Most comets are too far away to be seen from the Earth. They circle the Sun a thousand times farther away than the planet Neptune.

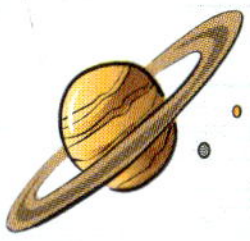

A comet may be only 15 kilometres across, but its tails can be millions of kilometres long.

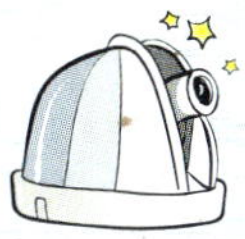

In 1908, a comet entered the Earth's atmosphere, then exploded over Siberia's Tunguska river. It flattened thousands of trees.

Asteroids

Many pieces of rock were left over when the Solar System formed. Thousands of them, from tiny grains to lumps nearly 1,000 kilometres wide, still orbit the Sun. Together they form the asteroid belt, a broad band of rocks between Mars and Jupiter.

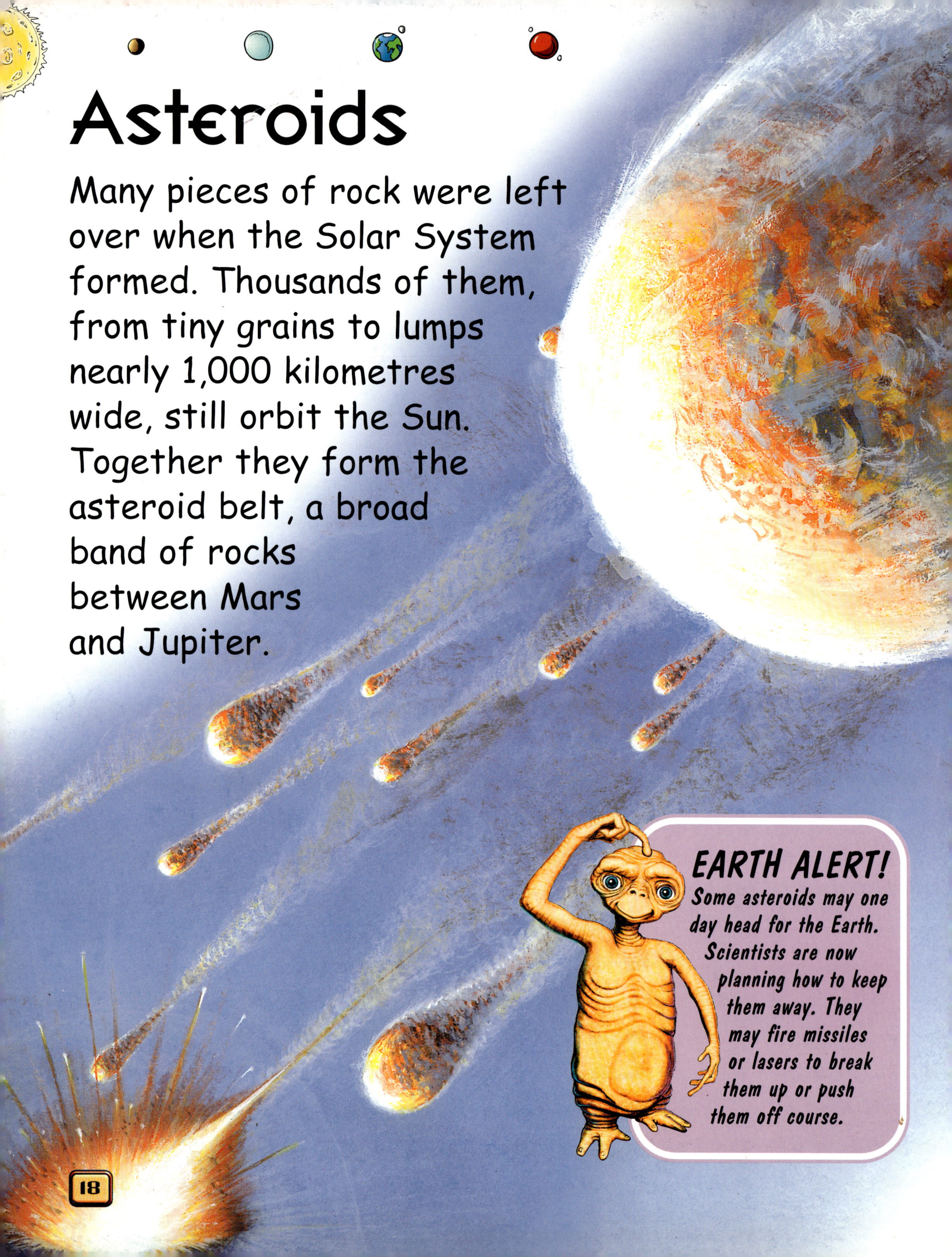

EARTH ALERT!

Some asteroids may one day head for the Earth. Scientists are now planning how to keep them away. They may fire missiles or lasers to break them up or push them off course.

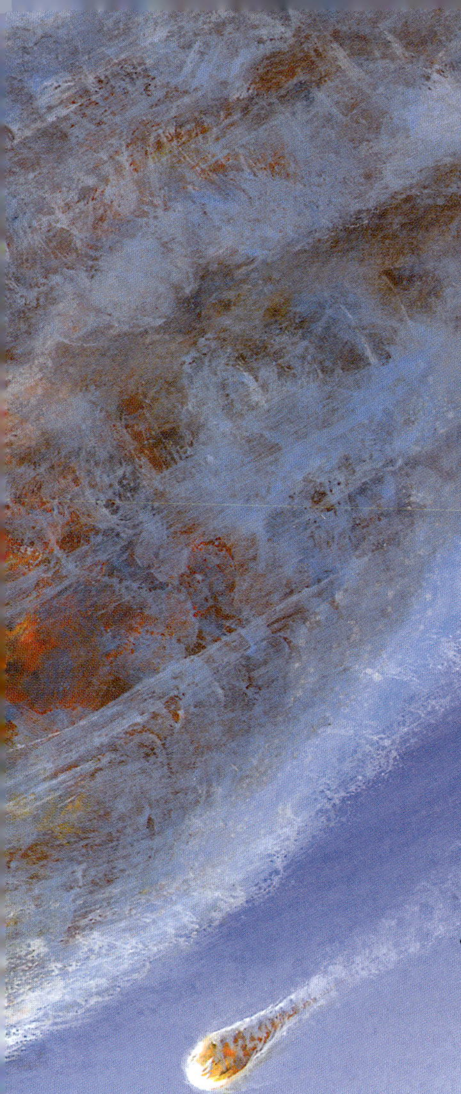

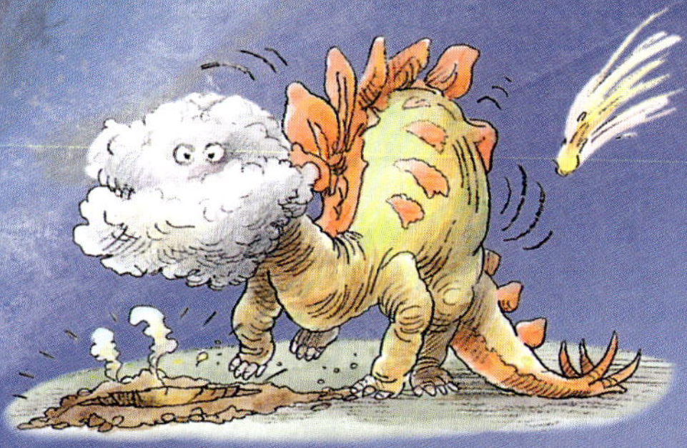

About 65 million years ago, a large asteroid hit the Earth near Mexico. The dust it threw up into the air blocked out the Sun's light for months. This may have killed the dinosaurs.

Belt of stone

The asteroid belt is about 165 million kilometres across. That is wider than the distance between the Earth and the Sun. Asteroids in the belt take three to six years to go round the Sun once. They all move from west to east, like the planets.

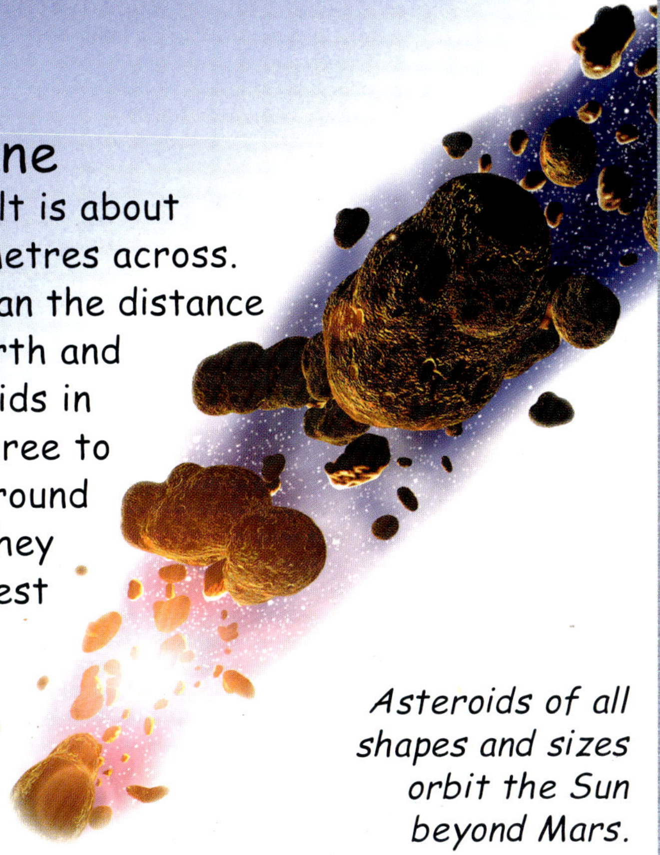

Asteroids of all shapes and sizes orbit the Sun beyond Mars.

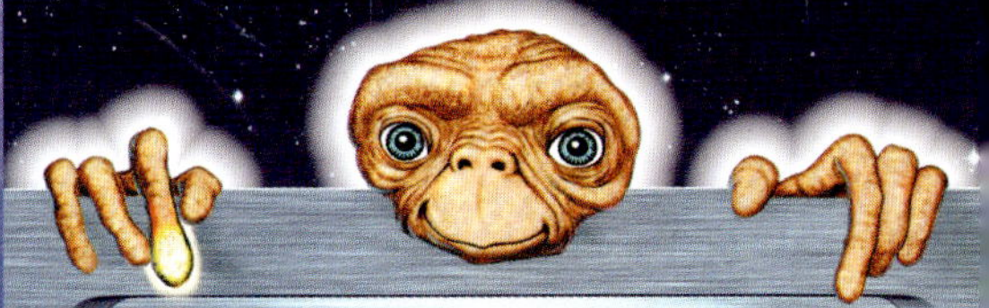

INFORMATION OVERLOAD!

E.T. has collected so many fascinating facts that he must send them back to his planet to be analysed.

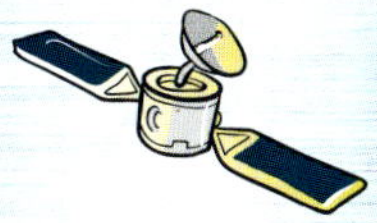

Scientists discovered the first asteroid 200 years ago and called it Ceres. It is still the biggest asteroid known.

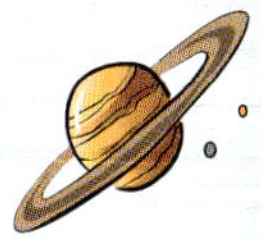

Most asteroids are in the asteroid belt, but two groups called Trojans have the same orbit as Jupiter.

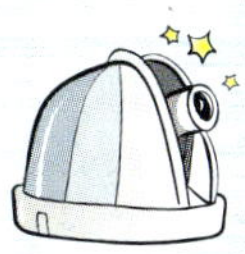

If all the asteroids were stuck together, they would make a planet 1,000 times smaller than the Earth.

Meteors and Meteorites

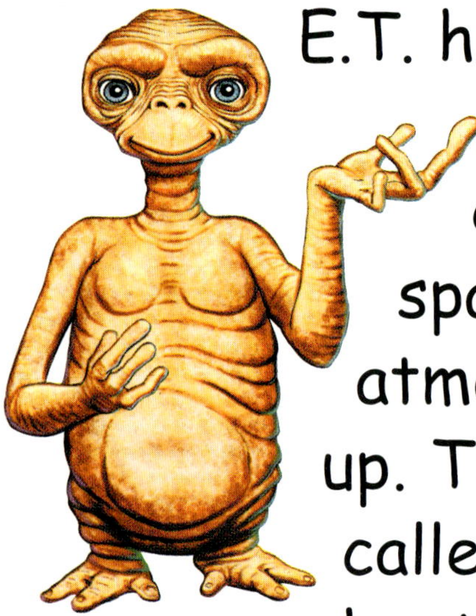

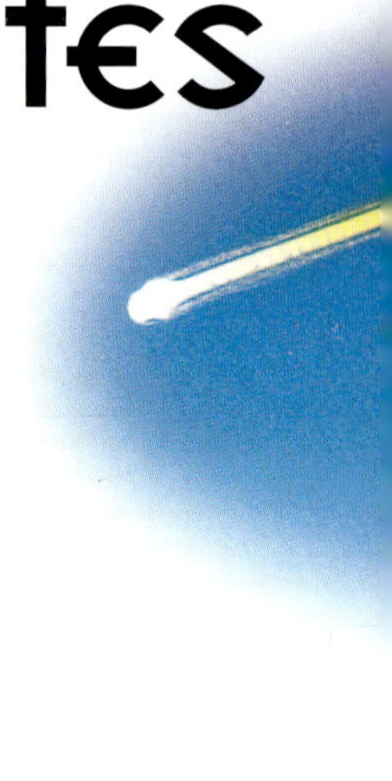

E.T. has seen streaks of light in the night sky. They are caused by dust specks from space flying into the Earth's atmosphere, then burning up. These objects are called meteors or shooting stars. Larger pieces of space rock that reach the ground are called meteorites.

PHONE HOME FACTS

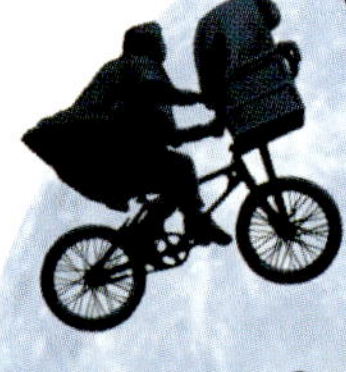

The biggest meteorite ever found is the 55-tonne Hoba West meteorite. It was discovered in Namibia, south-west Africa in 1920.

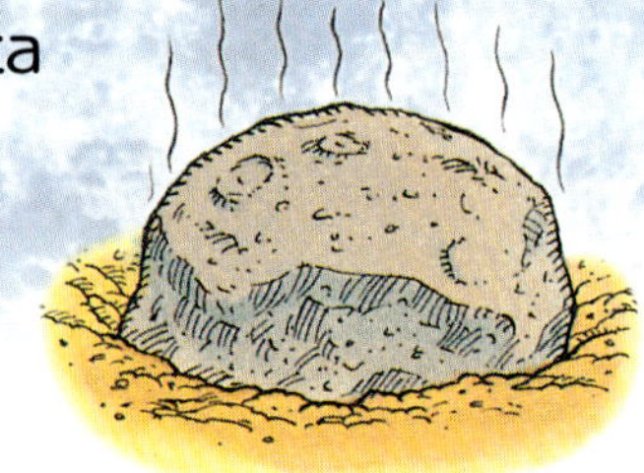

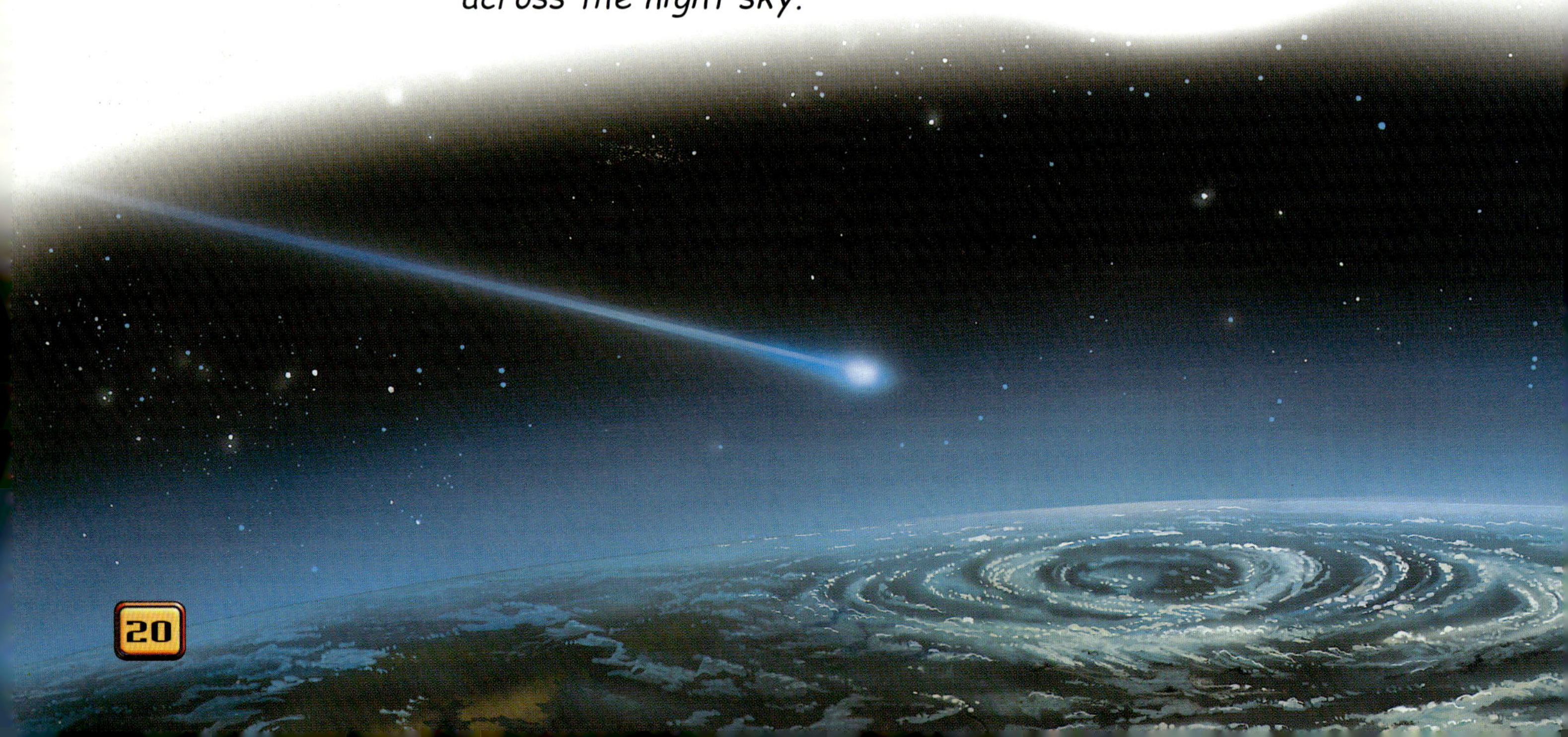

A meteor streaks across the night sky.

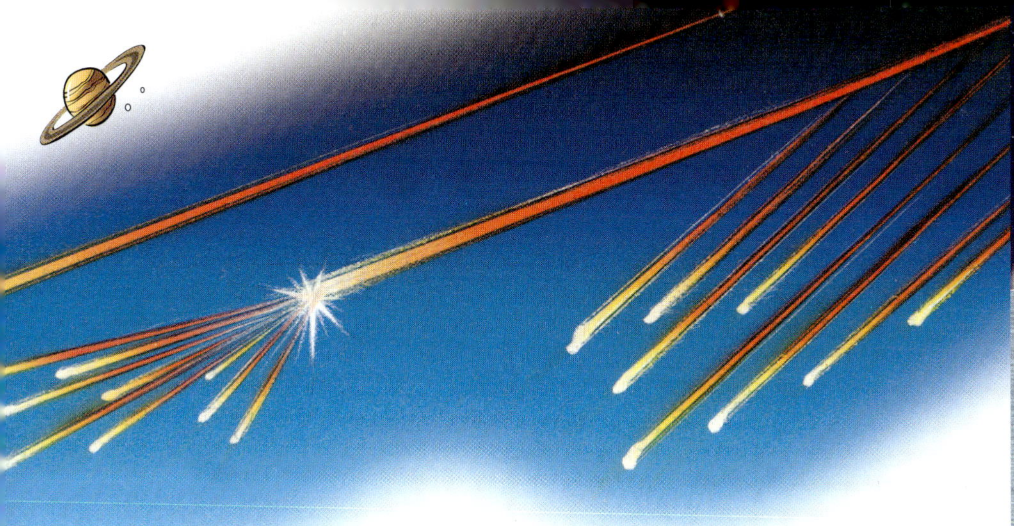

Meteor showers

You can see lots of meteors on certain nights every year. These 'meteor showers' happen when the Earth passes through the trail of dust left behind by a comet.

A big hole

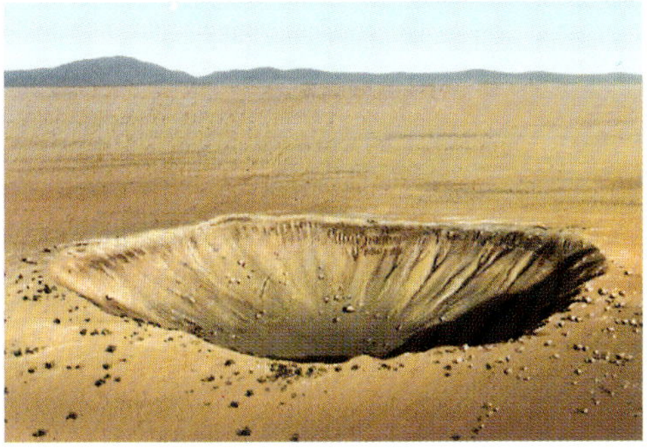

Meteor Crater in Arizona, USA, is about 50,000 years old. It formed when an iron meteorite weighing as much as 1,400 elephants slammed into the ground. The crater is 1,200 metres wide and 180 metres deep.

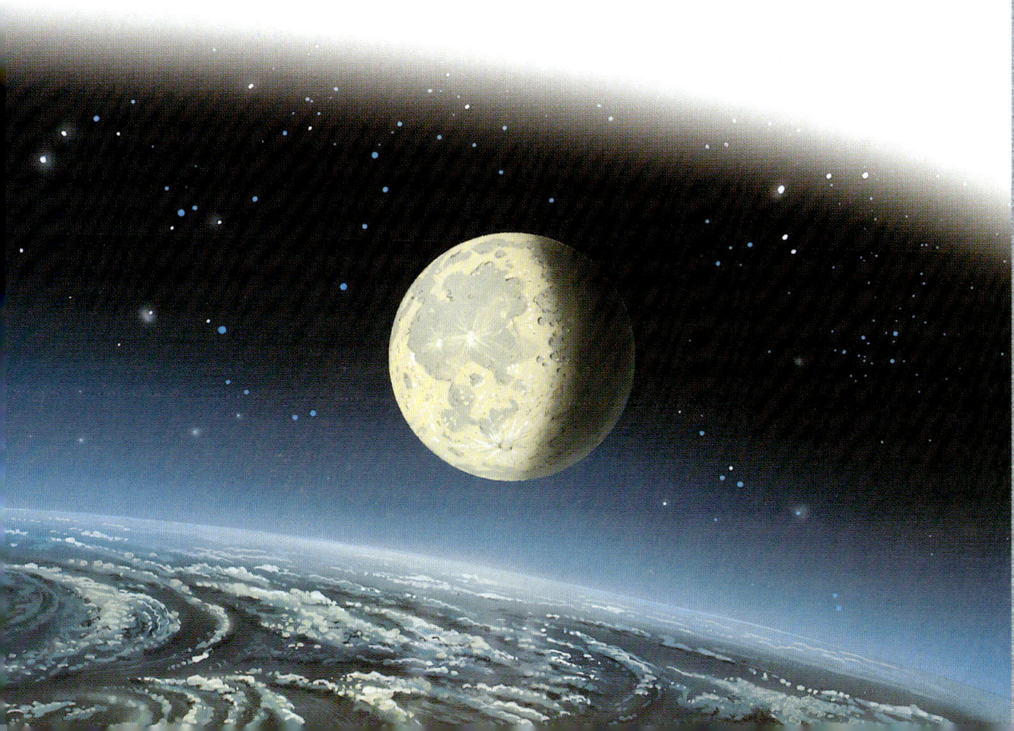

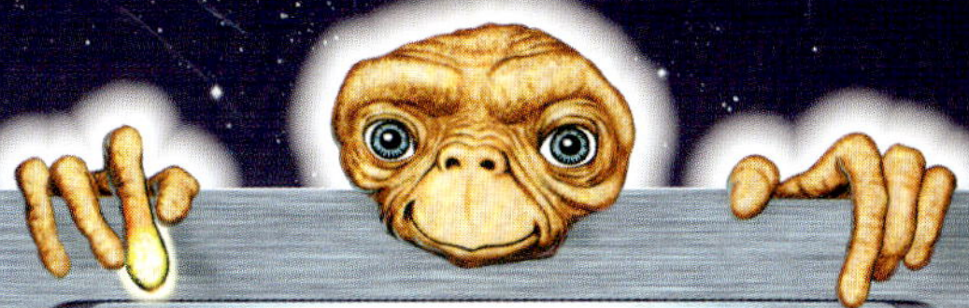

INFORMATION OVERLOAD!

E.T. has collected so many fascinating facts that he must send them back to his planet to be analysed.

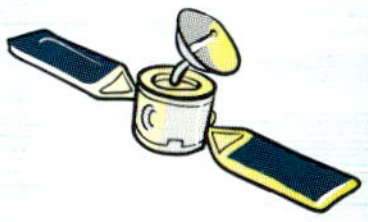

There are three main types of meteorite. They are made from stone, iron or a mixture of stone and iron.

A few meteorites are rocks that blasted away from the surfaces of the Moon and Mars when they were hit by other meteorites.

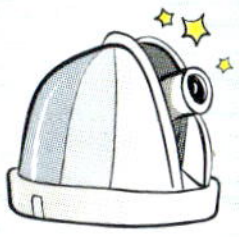

If somebody collected together all the dust that causes meteors every year, it would weigh up to 10,000 tonnes.

Space Travel

To travel into space without falling back to the Earth, E.T.'s spacecraft has to reach a speed of 11 kilometres a second. This is 40 times faster than a jumbo jet. Only rocket engines can produce this huge speed.

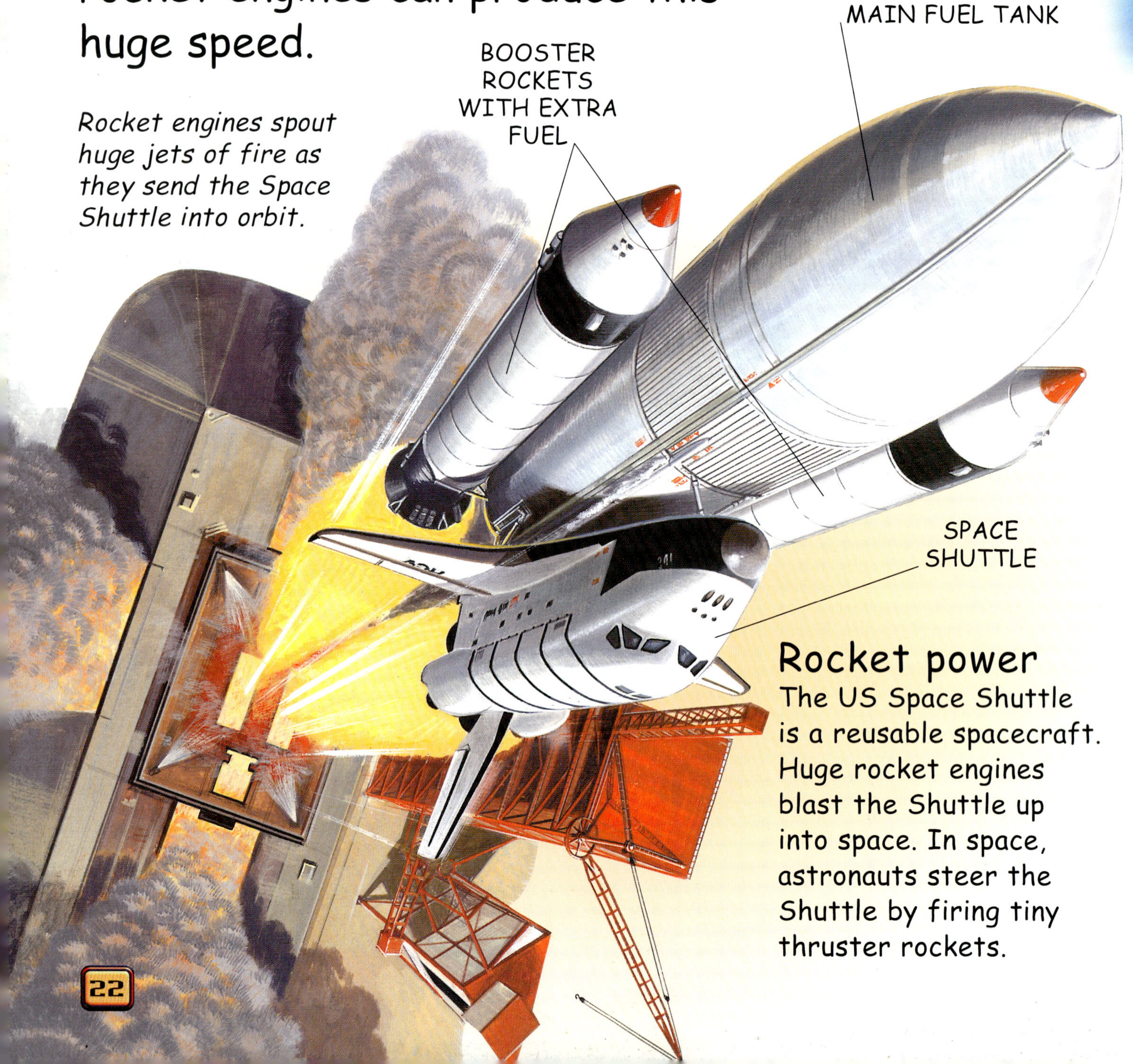

Rocket engines spout huge jets of fire as they send the Space Shuttle into orbit.

Rocket power

The US Space Shuttle is a reusable spacecraft. Huge rocket engines blast the Shuttle up into space. In space, astronauts steer the Shuttle by firing tiny thruster rockets.

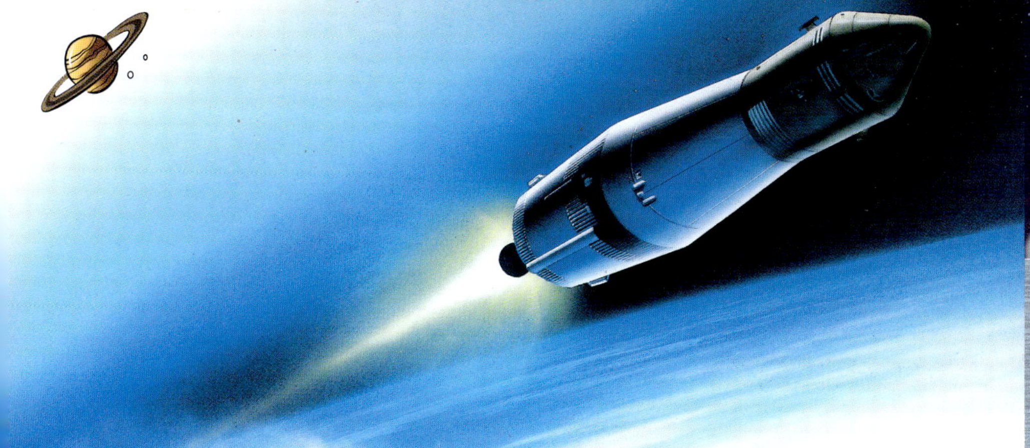

The Saturn V rocket took US astronauts to the Moon. It had three sections, called stages, on top of each other. When one stage used up its fuel, it fell away and the next stage took over.

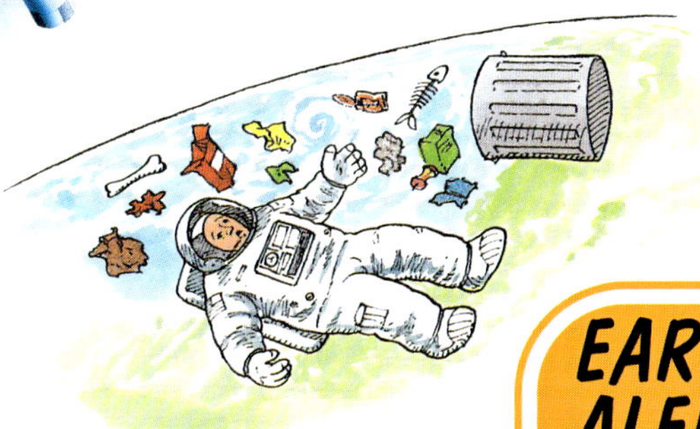

People have left lots of junk in space, including old satellites.

EARTH ALERT!

Space junk is dangerous as it could hit a spacecraft. The US Air Force tracks the biggest pieces so that spacecraft can avoid them.

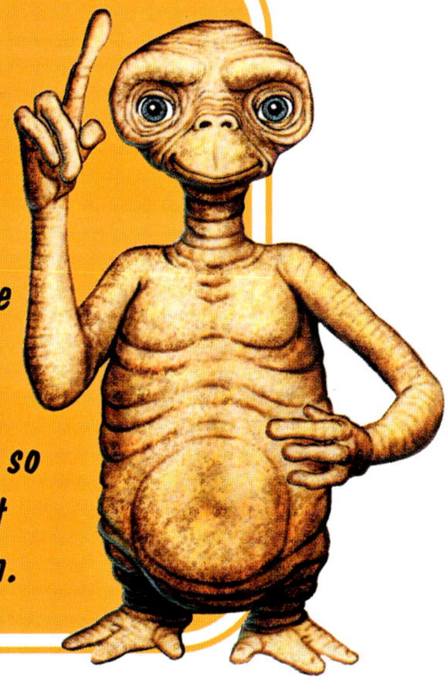

Back to the Earth

In the past, astronauts landed their spacecraft using parachutes to slow them down. US spacecraft landed in the Pacific Ocean, Russian spacecraft in Russia. But the Shuttle lands on a runway like a plane.

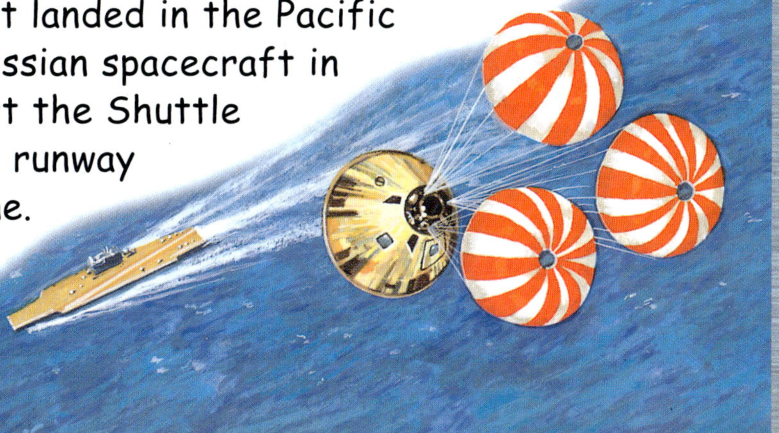

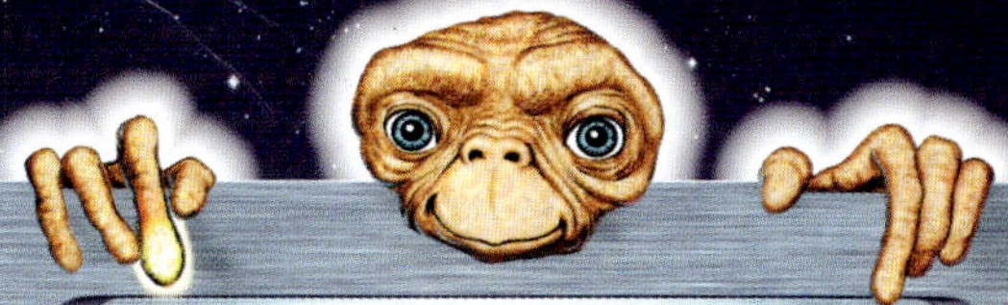

INFORMATION OVERLOAD!

E.T. has collected so many fascinating facts that he must send them back to his planet to be analysed.

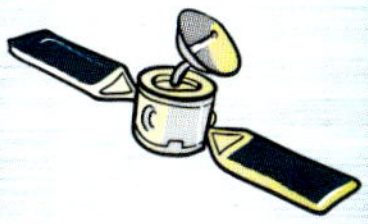

A satellite is any object that orbits a planet. The Space Age began on October 4, 1957, when scientists launched the first satellite made by people.

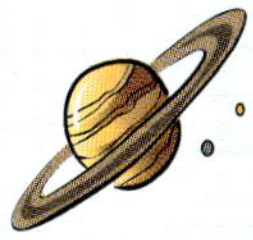

The first living creature to travel into space was a dog called Laika. In 1957, she orbited the Earth inside the Soviet spacecraft *Sputnik 2*.

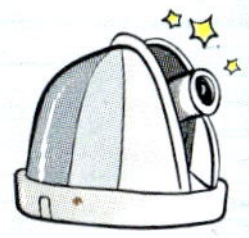

The first person to travel into space was Soviet Yuri Gagarin. In 1961, he made one orbit of the Earth in his *Vostok* space capsule.

Living in Space

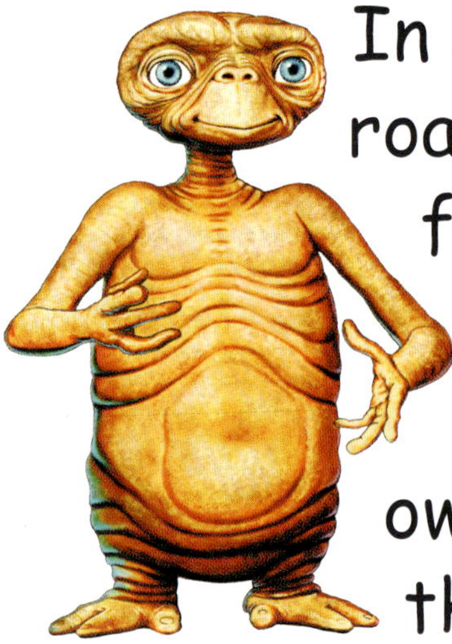

In space there is no air, it is roasting hot in the Sun and freezing cold in the dark. To live in space, humans – and E.T. – have to take their own warm atmosphere with them. They must also take all the food and drink they will need.

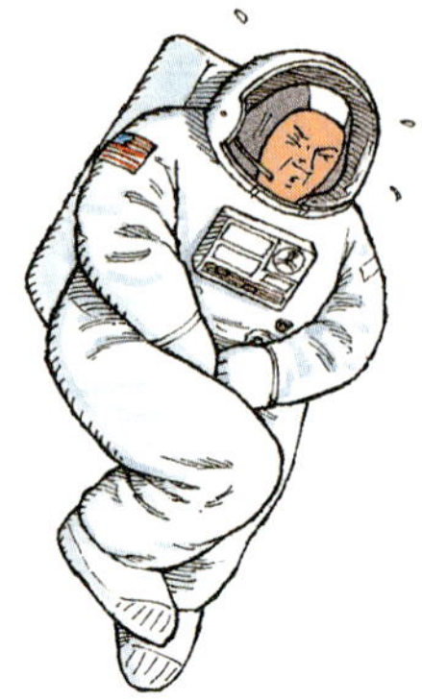

Astronauts use special space toilets. They suck the waste away.

Space stations

Astronauts can live and do experiments on board spacecraft called space stations. Some are already living on board the first part of a new International Space Station. One day, it will look like this.

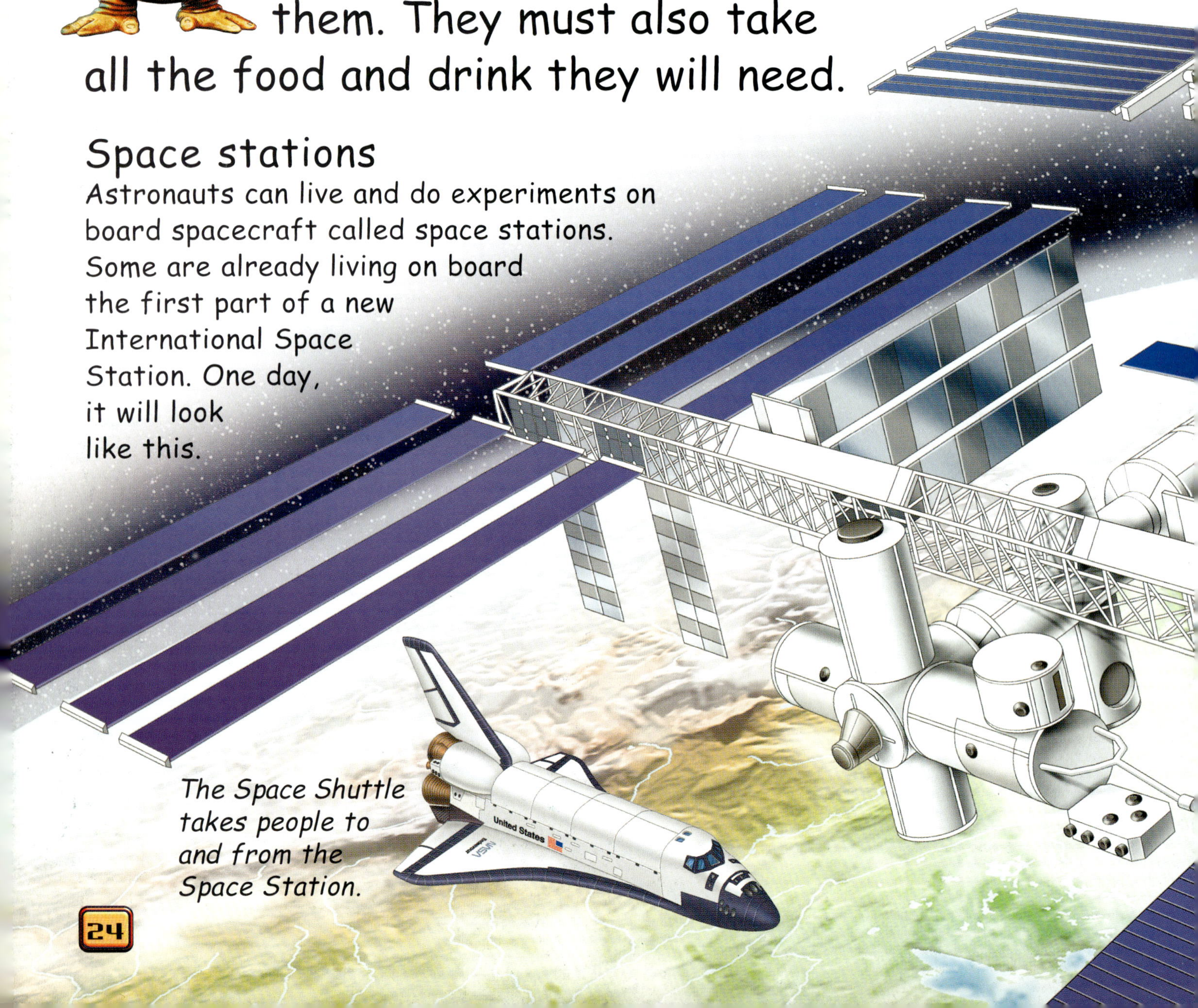

The Space Shuttle takes people to and from the Space Station.

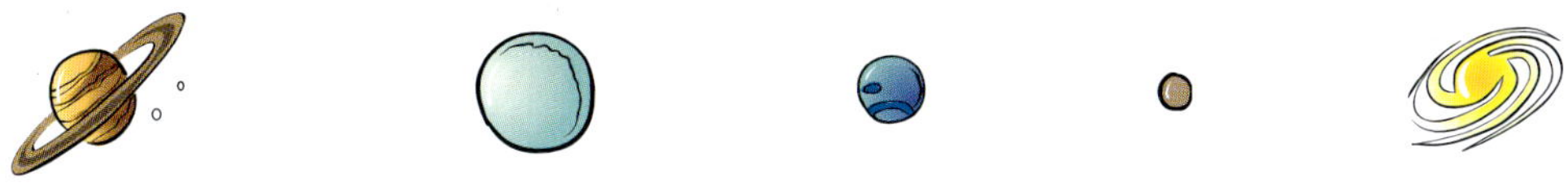

Inside and outside

Inside a spacecraft in orbit around the Earth, astronauts float about as if they weigh nothing. Outside a spacecraft, there is no air, and no heat in the shadows. So astronauts there must wear spacesuits that provide warmth, air to breathe and a radio to talk to other people.

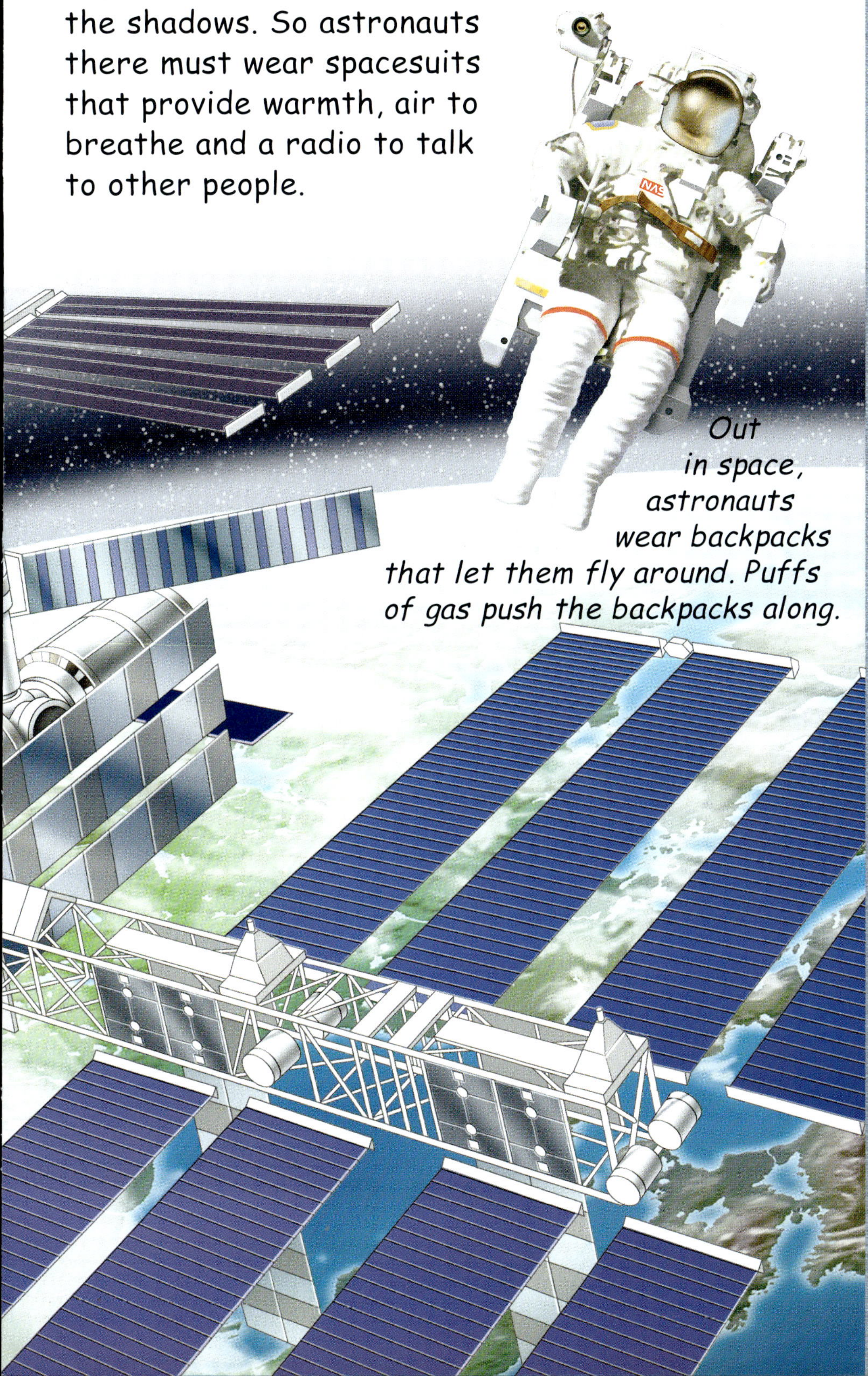

Out in space, astronauts wear backpacks that let them fly around. Puffs of gas push the backpacks along.

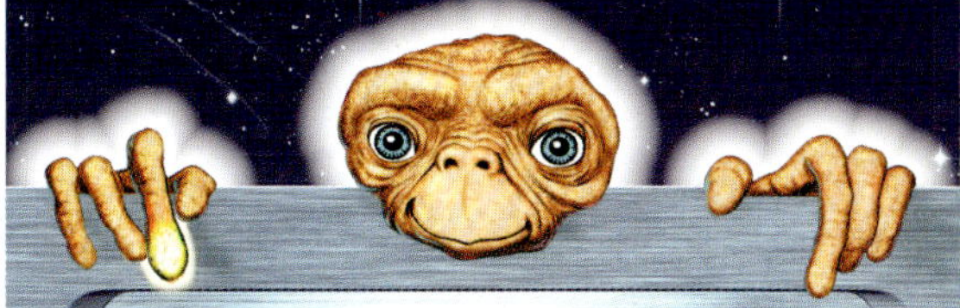

INFORMATION OVERLOAD!

E.T. has collected so many fascinating facts that he must send them back to his planet to be analysed.

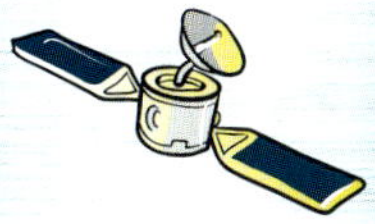

The longest ever spaceflight was made by Soviet Valeriy Poliyakov. He lived in the Mir space station from January 1994 to March 1995.

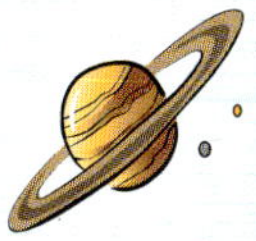

In 1969, the crew of the US *Apollo 10* spacecraft travelled at 39,897 kilometres an hour. No one has ever gone faster.

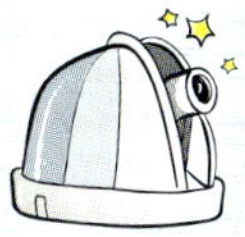

In March 1995, there were 13 people in space at the same time. This is the most people ever.

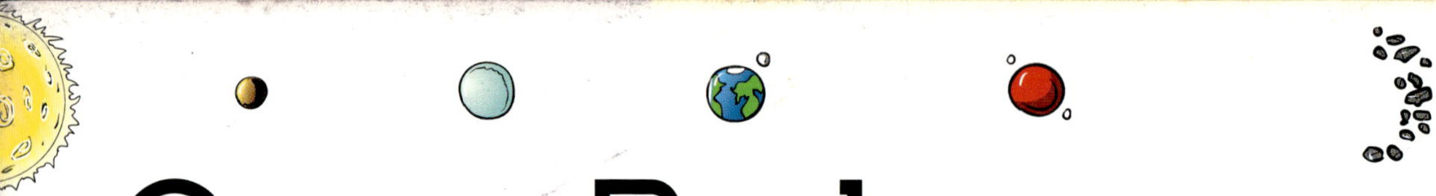

Space Probes

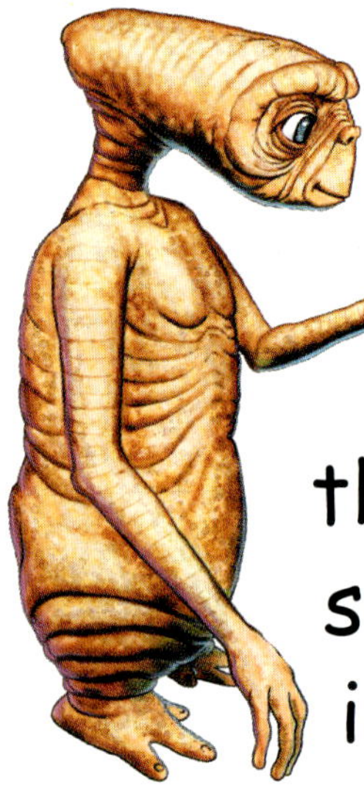

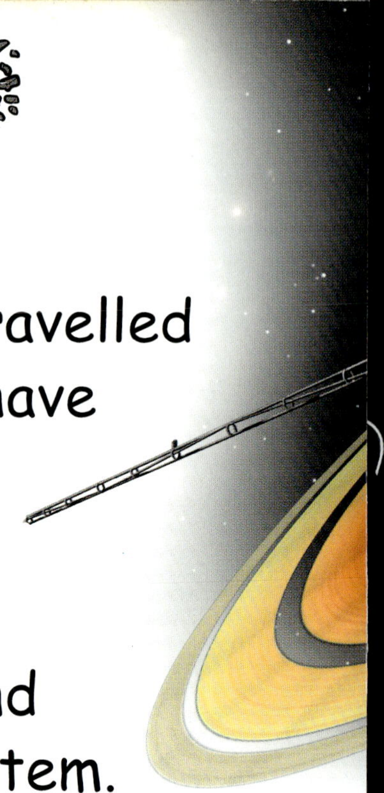

Unlike E.T., humans have not travelled to other planets. But they have sent spacecraft called probes to study most of them. The space probes have sent back lots of photographs and information about the Solar System.

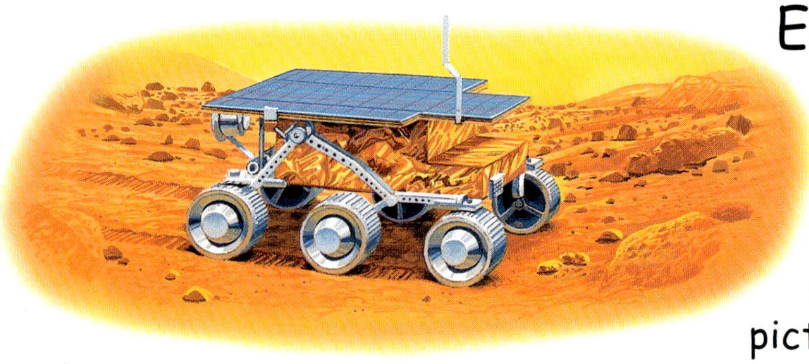

Exploring Mars

In 1997, the US *Pathfinder* space probe landed on Mars. It carried a vehicle called *Sojourner*. *Sojourner* moved around testing rocks and sending pictures back to the Earth.

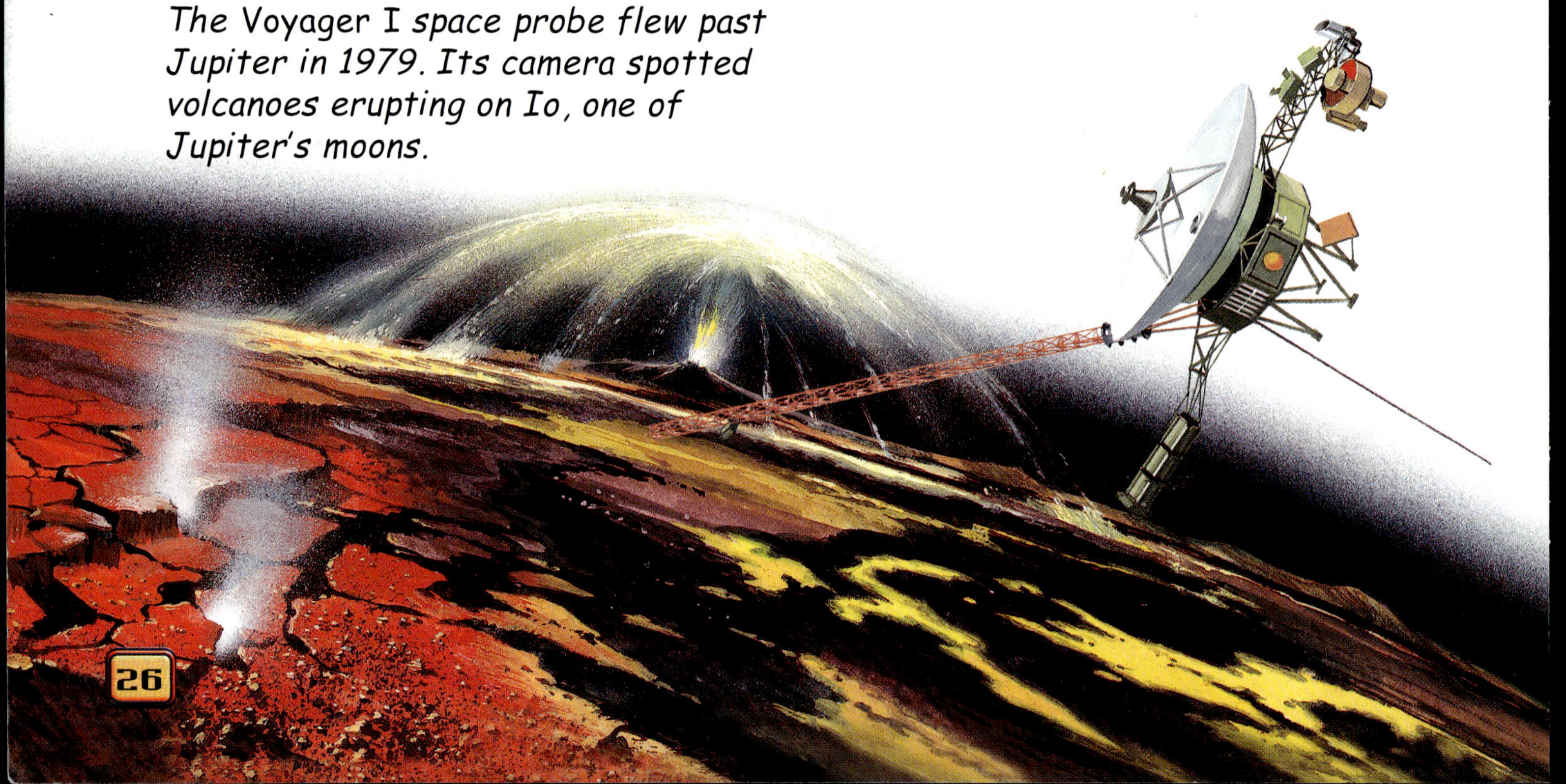

The Voyager I *space probe flew past Jupiter in 1979. Its camera spotted volcanoes erupting on Io, one of Jupiter's moons.*

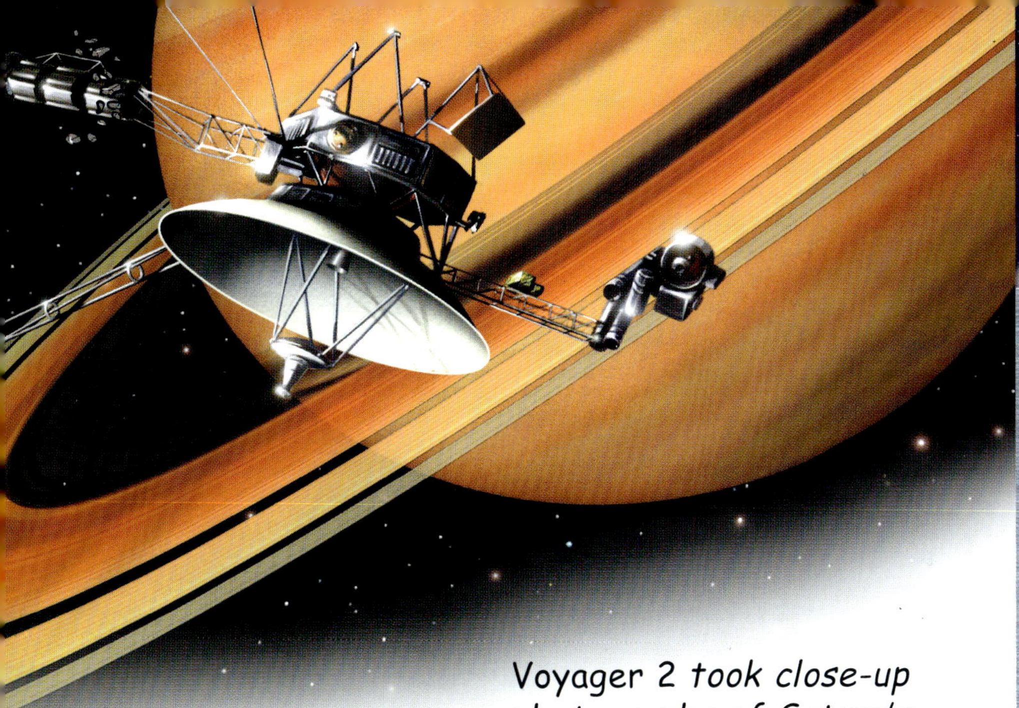

Voyager 2 took close-up photographs of Saturn's rings. They showed that the wide rings are made from lots of thinner rings.

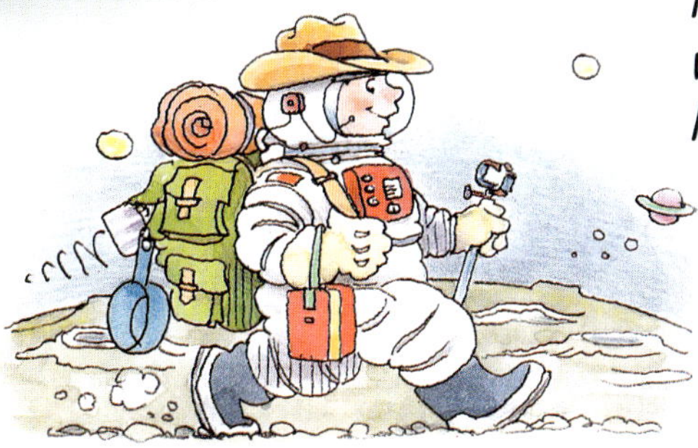

Astronauts are like explorers who once discovered unknown lands on the Earth. But people cannot yet travel to other planets, so space probes explore for us instead.

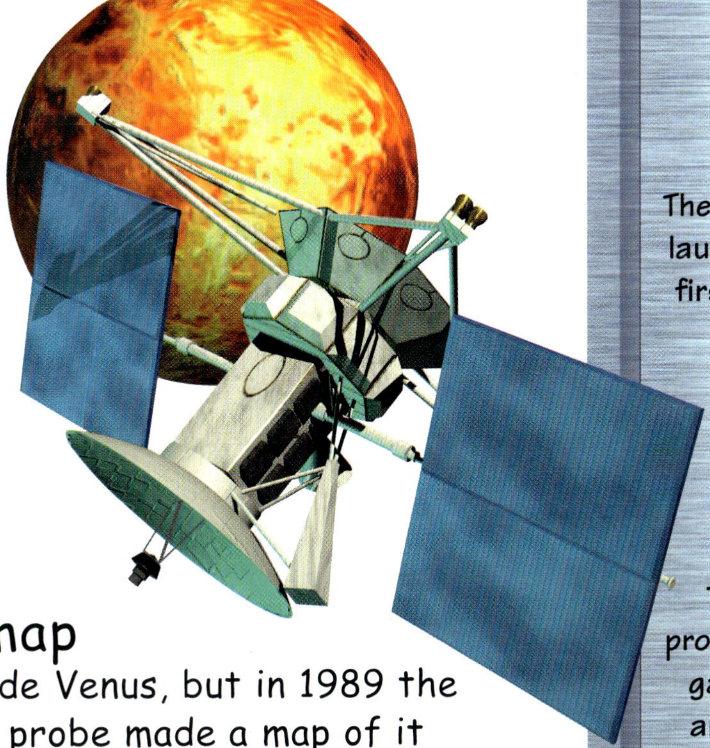

Magellan map

Thick clouds hide Venus, but in 1989 the *Magellan* space probe made a map of it by bouncing radio signals off its surface. The signals passed through the clouds.

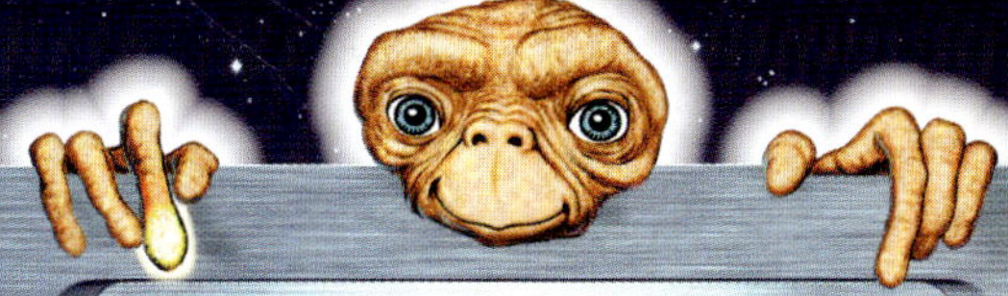

INFORMATION OVERLOAD!

E.T. has collected so many fascinating facts that he must send them back to his planet to be analysed.

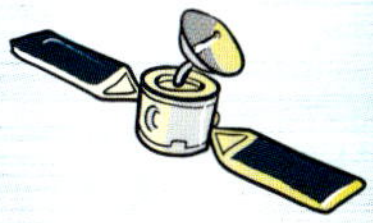

Space probes have landed on or flown past every planet in the Solar System except far-distant Pluto.

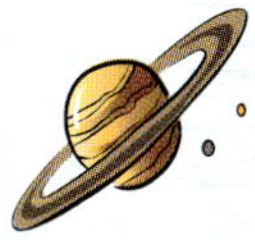

The US probe *Pioneer 10* was launched in 1972. It was the first to cross the asteroid belt and visit the outer planets.

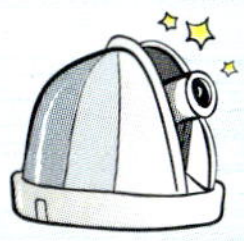

The two *Voyager* space probes explored all the giant gas planets in the 1970s and 1980s, then left the Solar System.

Searching for Extra-terrestrials

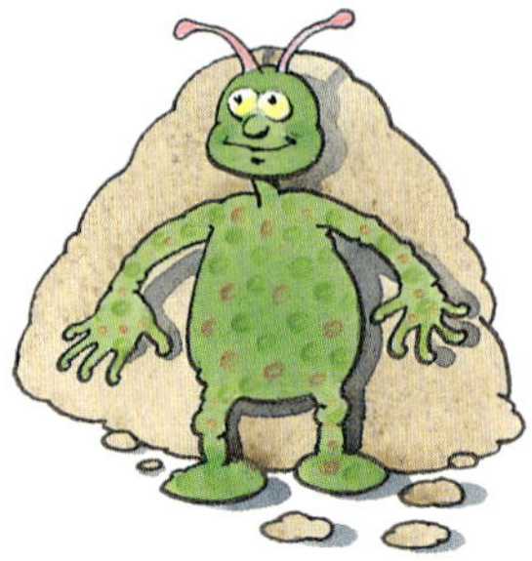

Scientists no longer expect to find beings like this in the Solar System.

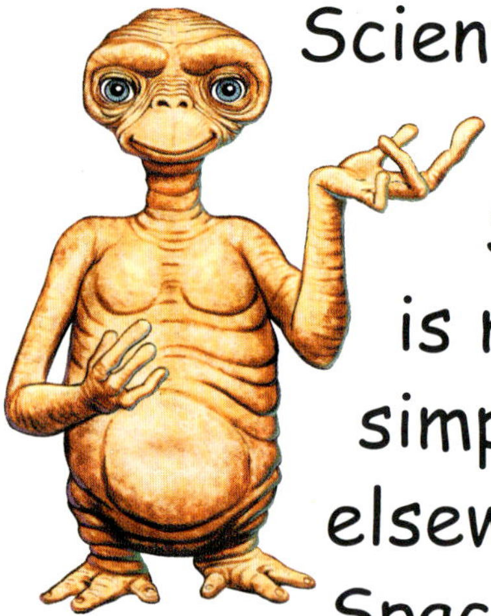

Scientists know that no creatures even a bit like us live in our Solar System – E.T.'s home is much farther away. But simple forms of life may exist elsewhere in the Solar System. Spacecraft are looking for them.

Titan

Saturn's moon Titan has a nitrogen-rich atmosphere like the Earth, and may have all the chemicals needed for life. In 2004, the *Cassini* space probe will drop a mini-probe called *Huygens* on to Titan to study it closely.

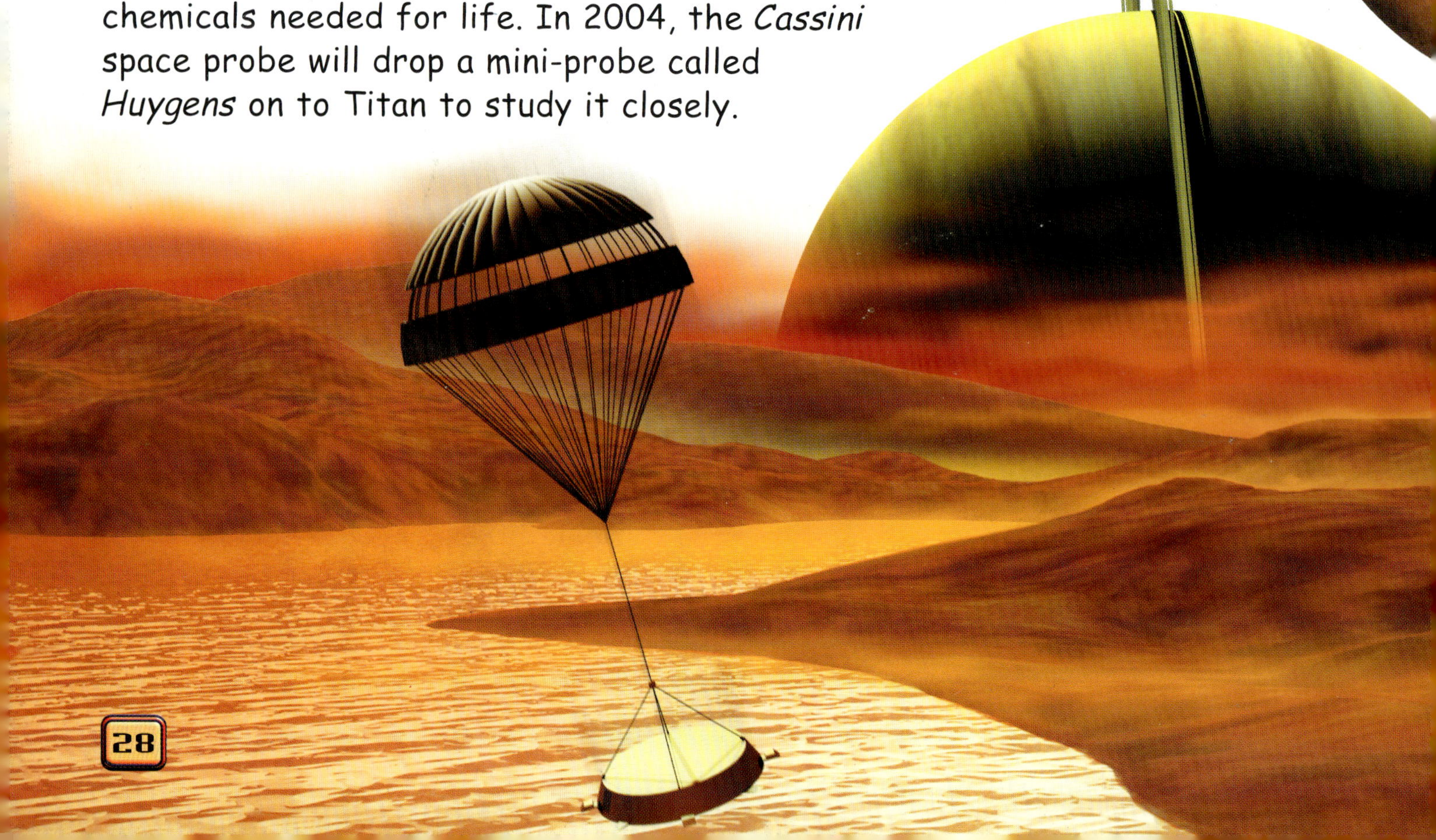

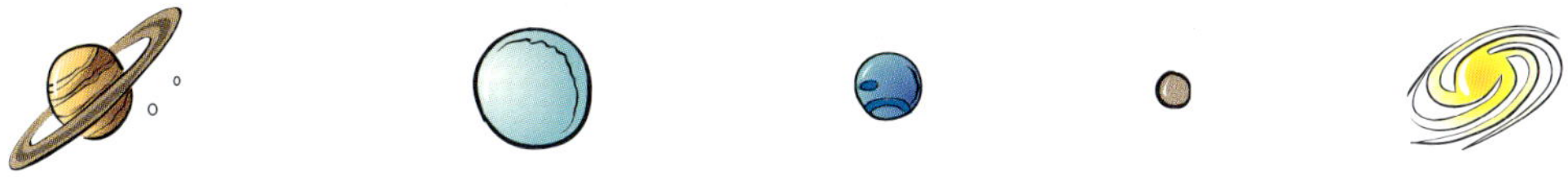

Europa

Jupiter's moon Europa is covered with ice. There may be water underneath. Where there is water, there may be life.

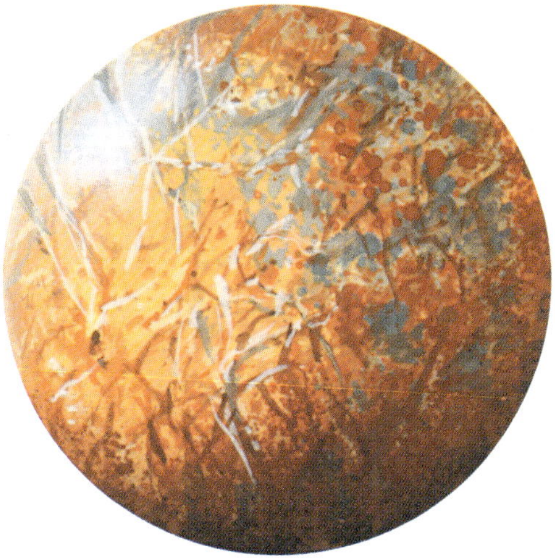

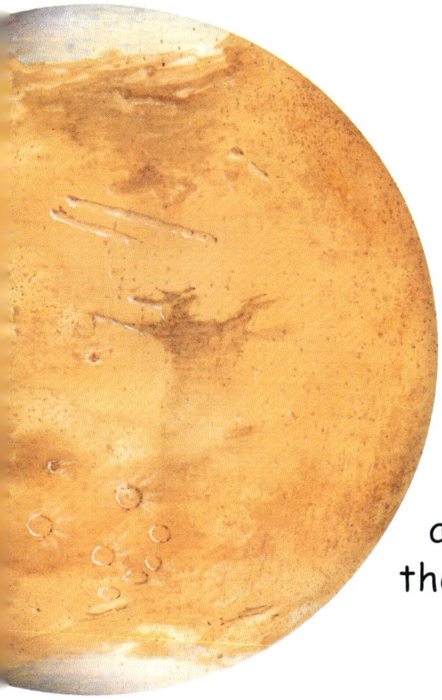

Life on Mars?

About 100 years ago, an astronomer said he had seen canals on Mars. He thought Martians had built them to carry water. The first close-up photographs of Mars, taken by a spacecraft in 1965, proved there are no canals after all.

In 1976, the US space probes Viking 1 and 2 went to Mars to look for life. Robot landers tested the soil, but could not prove life exists there.

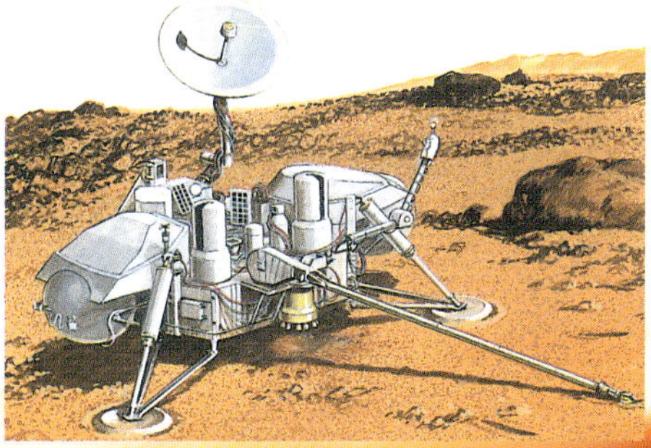

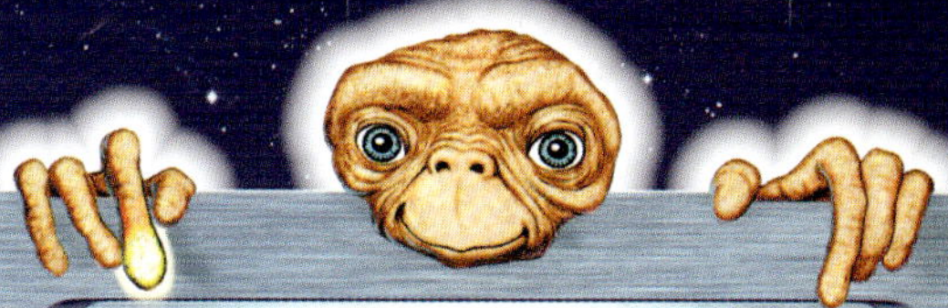

INFORMATION OVERLOAD!

E.T. has collected so many fascinating facts that he must send them back to his planet to be analysed.

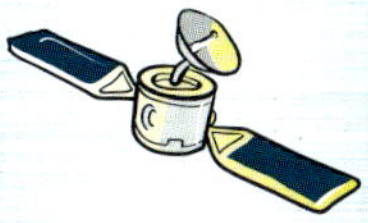

Scientists discovered tiny wormlike shapes inside one meteorite from Mars. Some scientists believe that these were once alive, but many others do not agree.

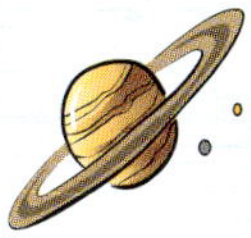

Scientists think there may be water, and life, under Mars' surface. The British *Beagle II* spacecraft will visit the planet in 2003 to check.

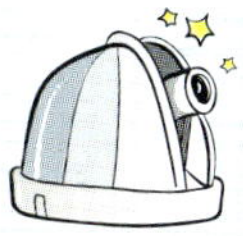

When the first astronauts returned from the Moon, scientists searched them for 'moon bugs'.

GOING HOME

E.T. has found out all he needs to know about the Solar System and now he is ready to go home. Help him get back to his spaceship.

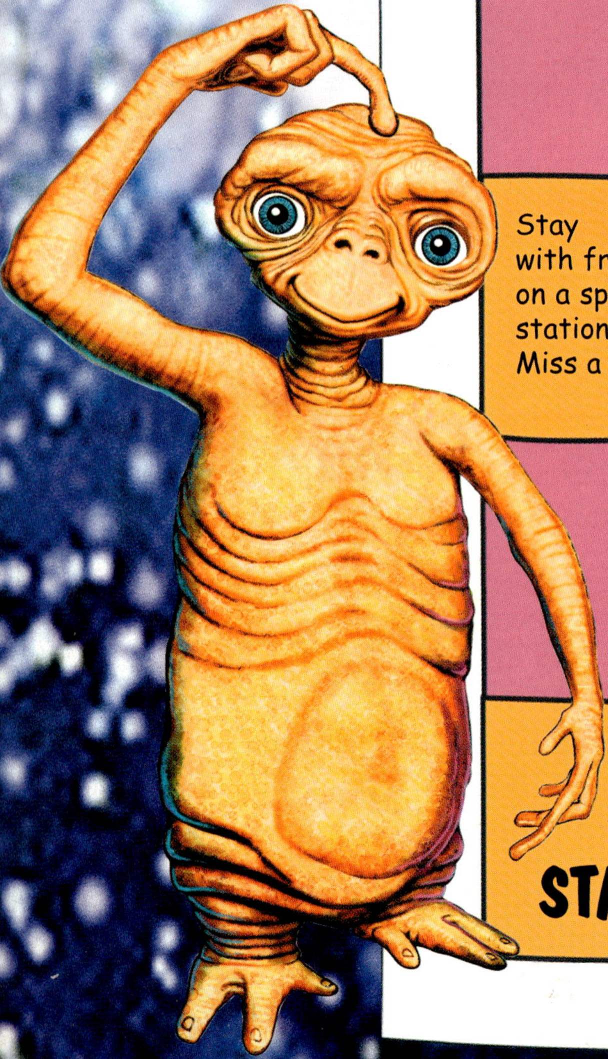

40 New galaxy expands. Move on 1 space. 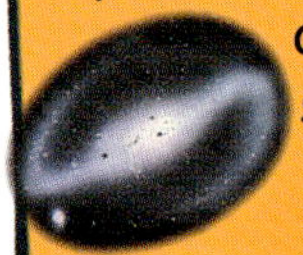	41	42 Break the rocket speed record. Move to 43. 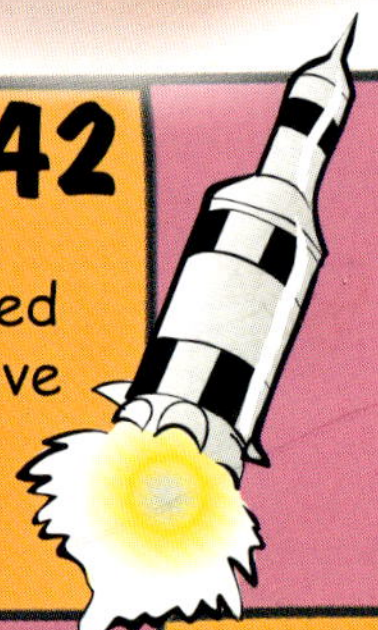	43
39	38 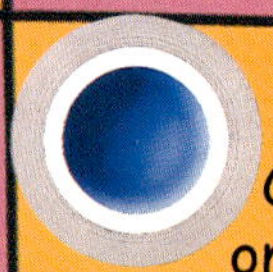 Caught on the rolling orbit of Uranus. Roll the dice again.	37	36 What do you get if you cross a galaxy with a toad? Star Warts!
20 Stay with friends on a space station. Miss a turn.	21	22 Catch a ride on a comet. Go on to 24.	23
19	18 If athletes get athlete's foot, what do astronauts get? Missile-toe.	17	16
START	1 Find a new star. Move up to 17. 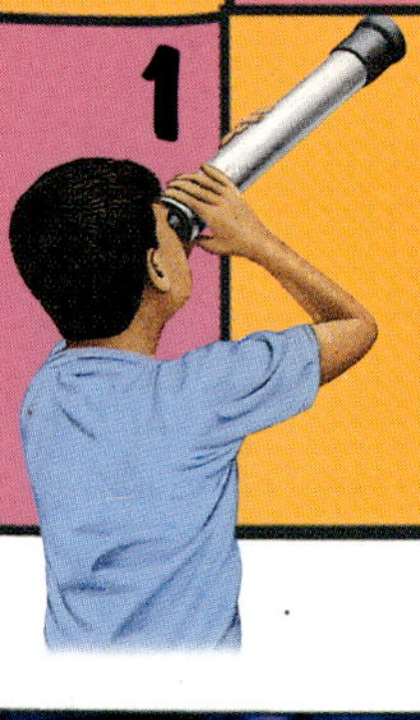	2	3 What do you call a mad astronaut? An astronut.

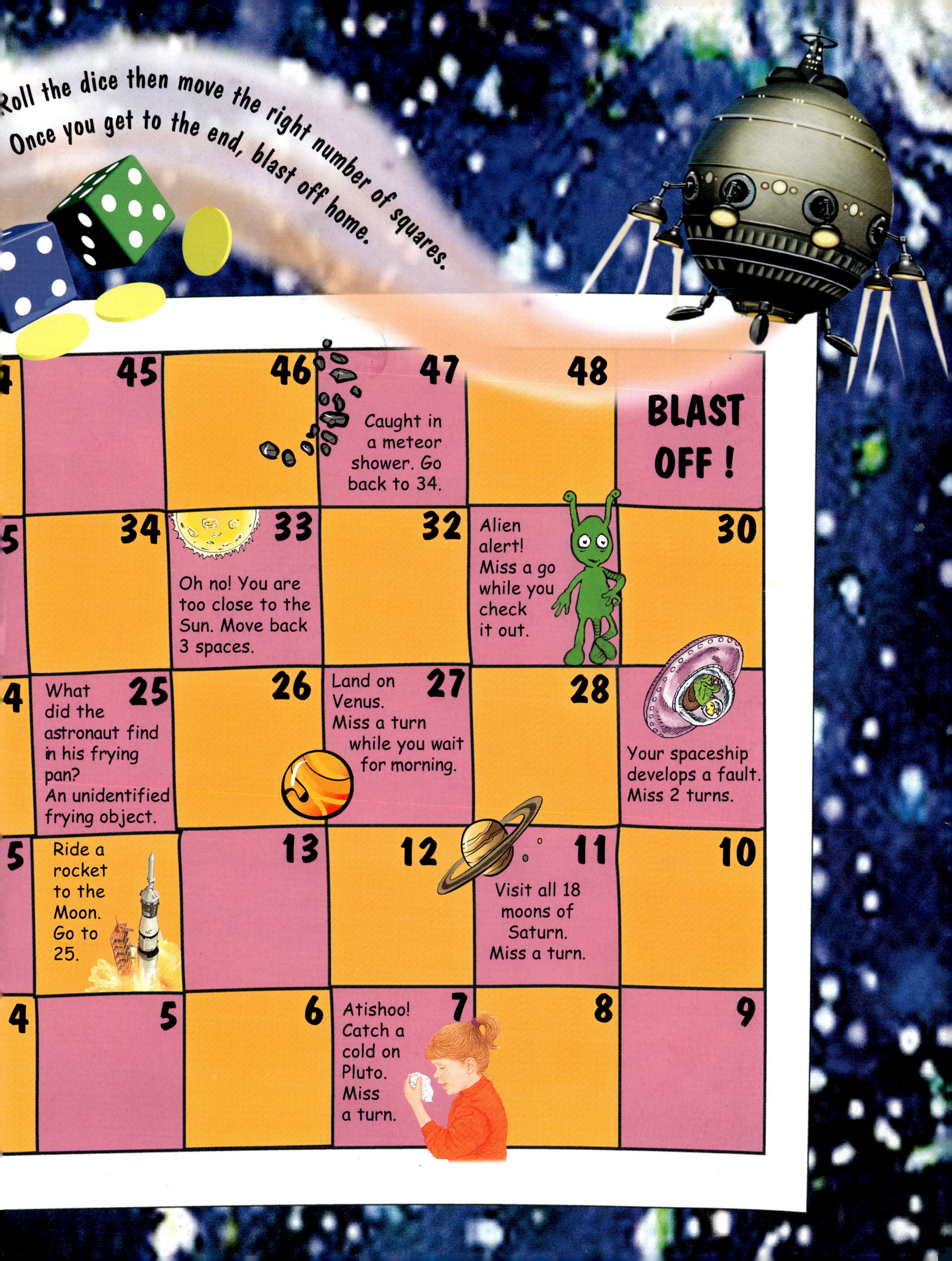

Roll the dice then move the right number of squares.
Once you get to the end, blast off home.
45
46
47
Caught in a meteor shower. Go back to 34.
48
BLAST OFF !
34
33
Oh no! You are too close to the Sun. Move back 3 spaces.
32
Alien alert! Miss a go while you check it out.
30
25
What did the astronaut find in his frying pan? An unidentified frying object.
26
27
Land on Venus. Miss a turn while you wait for morning.
28
Your spaceship develops a fault. Miss 2 turns.
13
12
11
Visit all 18 moons of Saturn. Miss a turn.
10
Ride a rocket to the Moon. Go to 25.
5
6
7
Atishoo! Catch a cold on Pluto. Miss a turn.
8
9

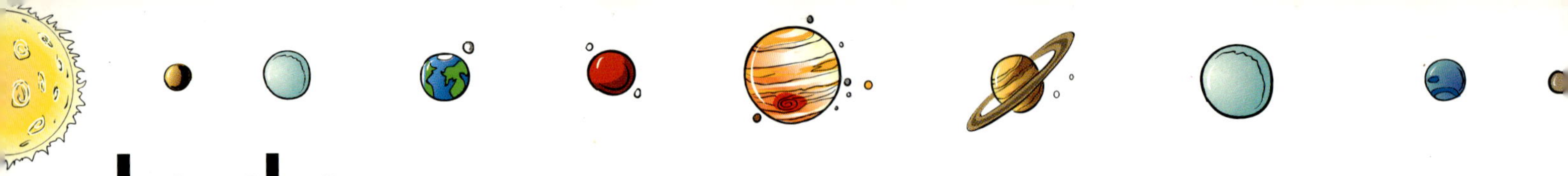

Index

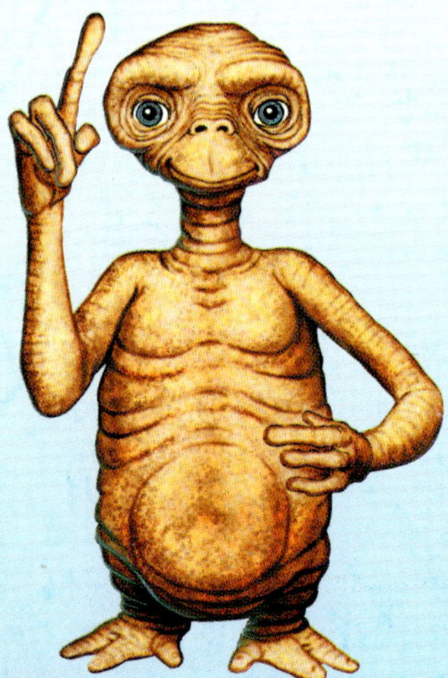